MICHAEL APPERWIND

THE SELF-CARE REVOLUTION

Transforming Your Mental Health Through Daily Rituals

Copyright © 2024 by MICHAEL APPERWIND

All rights reserved. No part of this publication may be reproduced, stored or transmitted in any form or by any means, electronic, mechanical, photocopying, recording, scanning, or otherwise without written permission from the publisher. It is illegal to copy this book, post it to a website, or distribute it by any other means without permission.

MICHAEL APPERWIND asserts the moral right to be identified as the author of this work.

MICHAEL APPERWIND has no responsibility for the persistence or accuracy of URLs for external or third-party Internet Websites referred to in this publication and does not guarantee that any content on such Websites is, or will remain, accurate or appropriate.

Designations used by companies to distinguish their products are often claimed as trademarks. All brand names and product names used in this book and on its cover are trade names, service marks, trademarks and registered trademarks of their respective owners. The publishers and the book are not associated with any product or vendor mentioned in this book. None of the companies referenced within the book have endorsed the book.

First edition

This book was professionally typeset on Reedsy.
Find out more at reedsy.com

Contents

Introduction   1

1   Chapter 1: The Foundation of Self-Care   5

2   Chapter 2: Morning Rituals for a Positive Start   11

3   Chapter 3: Daytime Rituals for Stress Management   21

4   Chapter 4: Evening Rituals for Restful Sleep   26

5   Chapter 5: Emotional Self-Care Rituals   32

6   Chapter 6: Physical Self-Care Rituals   38

7   Chapter 7: Social Self-Care Rituals   45

8   Chapter 8: Digital Detox Rituals   52

9   Chapter 9: Nature and Environmental Self-Care   59

10   Chapter 10: Spiritual Self-Care Rituals   66

11   Chapter 11: Creative Self-Care Rituals   73

12   Chapter 12: Professional Self-Care Rituals   79

13   Chapter 13: Customizing Your Self-Care Revolution   85

14   Sources Chapter 2   98

15   Sources Chapter 3:   100

16   Sources Chapter 4:   102

17   Sources Chapter 5:   105

18   Sources Chapter 7:   108

19   Sources Chapter 8:   111

20   Sources Chapter 9:   114

21   Sources Chapter 10:   118

22   Sources Chapter 11:   122

23   Sources Chapter 12:   125

24   Sources Chapter 13:   129

Introduction

The Self-Care Revolution: Transforming Your Mental Health Through Daily Rituals
   Introduction

1. The Mental Health Crisis and the Role of Self-Care

The world is facing an unprecedented mental health crisis. According to the World Health Organization, depression affects more than 264 million people globally, while anxiety disorders affect 284 million. The COVID-19 pandemic has exacerbated these issues, with a study published in The Lancet reporting a 25% increase in anxiety and depression worldwide in 2020 alone.

In the United States, the situation is equally concerning. The National Institute of Mental Health reports that nearly one in five U.S. adult's lives with a mental illness (52.9 million in 2020). More alarmingly, suicide rates have increased by 35% since 1999, making it the 10th leading cause of death in the U.S.

This crisis is not just about numbers; it's about human suffering. It affects productivity (costing the global economy US\$ 1 trillion per year in lost productivity), relationships, and overall quality of life. Traditional mental health services, while crucial, are often insufficient or inaccessible. In the U.S., 55% of counties have no psychiatrists, psychologists, or social workers.

Enter self-care. While not a replacement for professional help when needed, self-care offers a proactive, accessible approach to maintaining and improving mental health. It empowers individuals to take charge of their well-being, providing tools to manage stress, build resilience, and foster positive mental states. Studies have shown that consistent self-care practices can reduce the risk of mental health issues and improve outcomes for those already struggling.

1. Defining self-care: More than just bubble baths and face masks

Self-care has often been misrepresented in popular culture as indulgent pampering or expensive treats. While these can be elements of self-care, true self-care is far more comprehensive and fundamental to our well-being.

At its core, self-care is any activity we do deliberately to take care of our mental, emotional, and physical health. It's a multifaceted approach that includes:

- Physical self-care: Regular exercise, balanced nutrition, adequate sleep, and preventive healthcare.
- Emotional self-care: Practices that help us process and express our feelings healthily, such as journaling, therapy, or talking with friends.
- Mental self-care: Activities that keep our minds sharp and engaged, like learning new skills, solving puzzles, or reading.
- Social self-care: Nurturing our relationships and setting healthy boundaries.
- Spiritual self-care: Engaging in practices that nurture our spirit, whether through organized religion, meditation, or connecting with nature.
- Professional self-care: Setting work-life boundaries, taking breaks, and pursuing professional development.

Self-care is not selfish or indulgent; it's a necessary part of maintaining our health and well-being. It's about creating daily habits and rituals that support our overall functioning and help us navigate life's challenges more effectively.

For instance, a comprehensive self-care routine might include:

- Starting the day with a 10-minute meditation
- Taking regular breaks during work to stretch and move
- Eating a balanced lunch away from your desk
- Setting aside time for a hobby or creative pursuit
- Ending the day with a technology-free wind-down routine

These practices, when done consistently, can have a profound impact on our mental health and overall well-being.

1. The science behind how daily rituals can transform mental health

The transformative power of daily self-care rituals is rooted in neuroscience and psychology. Here's how these practices can literally change our brains and improve our mental health:

Neuroplasticity: Our brains have the ability to form new neural connections throughout our lives, a concept known as neuroplasticity. When we engage in regular self-care practices, we're creating and strengthening neural pathways associated with positive emotions, resilience, and well-being. A study published in Frontiers in Human Neuroscience found that eight weeks of daily meditation increased gray matter density in brain regions associated with learning, memory, and emotion regulation.

Stress Reduction: Many self-care practices activate the parasympathetic nervous system, our "rest and digest" mode. This counteracts the effects of chronic stress, which can be detrimental to mental health. For example, a study in Health Psychology showed that mindfulness meditation can lower cortisol levels, reducing the harmful effects of stress on the body and mind.

Neurotransmitter Balance: Self-care activities often boost the production of neurotransmitters associated with positive mood. Exercise, for instance, increases the release of endorphins, serotonin, and dopamine, our body's natural mood elevators. A study in the Journal of Psychiatry & Neuroscience found that regular exercise can be as effective as medication for some people with depression.

Improved Sleep: Many self-care practices, such as maintaining a consistent bedtime routine or practicing relaxation techniques, can improve sleep quality. Good sleep is crucial for mental health; a study in The Lancet Psychiatry found that people with disrupted sleep patterns were more likely to experience symptoms of depression and anxiety.

Enhanced Emotional Regulation: Regular self-care can improve our ability to manage emotions. Practices like mindfulness and journaling help us process emotions more effectively. A study in Emotion found that people who practiced mindfulness regularly showed greater activation in brain regions associated with emotional regulation when exposed to negative stimuli.

Cognitive Function: Engaging in mentally stimulating activities as part of self-care can enhance cognitive function and potentially reduce the risk of cognitive decline. A study in the Journal of Alzheimer's Disease found that engaging in cognitively stimulating activities was associated with a lower risk of mild cognitive impairment.

By understanding the science behind self-care, we can appreciate that these daily rituals are not just "feel-good" activities, but powerful tools for transforming our mental health at a neurobiological level. Consistent practice is key; these changes occur gradually over time as we build and reinforce healthier neural pathways.

$$1$$

Chapter 1: The Foundation of Self-Care

1. **Understanding the mind-body connection**

The concept of self-care is rooted in the profound interconnection between our minds and bodies. This relationship, studied in the field of psycho-neuroimmunology, reveals how our thoughts, emotions, and physical health are inextricably linked.

Consider the last time you felt stressed about a work deadline. Your heart may have raced, your palms might have become sweaty, and you may have experienced a knot in your stomach. These physical reactions are your body's response to mental stress. When we're under chronic stress, our bodies produce excess cortisol, often referred to as the "stress hormone." Elevated cortisol levels can lead to inflammation, weakened immune function, and even changes in brain structure over time.

Conversely, positive mental states can have beneficial effects on our physical health. Studies have shown that practices like meditation and mindfulness can lower blood pressure, reduce chronic pain, and even boost immune function. For instance, a 2003 study by Davidson et al. found that mindfulness meditation led to increased left-sided anterior activation in the brain, a pattern associated with positive affect and enhanced immune function.

1. **The impact of daily habits on mental health**

Our brains are remarkably adaptable, a quality known as neuroplasticity. This means that our repeated thoughts and actions can physically reshape our brains by creating and strengthening neural pathways.

Think of your brain as a vast forest. The thoughts and actions you repeat most often become well-worn paths through this forest. The more you use these paths, the easier they become to traverse. This is why habits, both good and bad, can feel so automatic over time.

For example, if you habitually respond to stress by reaching for unhealthy snacks, this pathway becomes stronger, making it your default response. However, if you consistently practice deep breathing when stressed, this healthier response will become your new default over time.

Some habits, known as "keystone habits," have a ripple effect on other areas of our lives. For instance, regular exercise often leads to better eating habits, improved sleep, and increased productivity. By focusing on these keystone habits, we can create positive cascades of change in our lives.

1. **Assessing your current self-care practices**

Before embarking on your self-care journey, it's crucial to understand your starting point. Let's take a moment to assess your current self-care practices across various life domains:

Self-Care Assessment Tool

Rate each item on a scale of 1 to 5, where 1 = Never, 2 = Rarely, 3 = Sometimes, 4 = Often, and 5 = Always.

Physical Health:

1. I engage in regular physical exercise (at least 150 minutes per week)
2. I maintain a balanced and nutritious diet
3. I get 7-9 hours of quality sleep each night
4. I stay hydrated throughout the day
5. I attend regular health check-ups and screenings

Emotional Well-being:

1. I practice stress-reduction techniques (e.g., deep breathing, meditation)
2. I express my emotions in healthy ways
3. I engage in activities that bring me joy and relaxation
4. I set and maintain healthy boundaries in my relationships
5. I seek professional help when needed (e.g., therapy, counseling)

Social Connections:

1. I maintain regular contact with friends and family
2. I have a support system I can rely on in times of need
3. I engage in meaningful social activities or group hobbies
4. I practice active listening and empathy in my relationships
5. I contribute to my community through volunteering or social engagement

Spiritual Practices:

1. I engage in activities that provide a sense of meaning or purpose

2. I practice mindfulness or meditation regularly
3. I spend time in nature or engage in activities that connect me to something greater than myself
4. I reflect on my values and align my actions with them
5. I engage in practices that nurture my spirit (e.g., prayer, yoga, art)

Professional Life:

1. I maintain a healthy work-life balance
2. I set clear boundaries between work and personal time
3. I engage in continuous learning and professional development
4. I take regular breaks during the workday to recharge
5. I feel a sense of purpose and satisfaction in my work

Scoring:

- 100-125: Excellent self-care practices
- 75-99: Good self-care practices with room for improvement
- 50-74: Moderate self-care practices; consider focusing on lower-scoring areas
- 25-49: Low self-care practices; prioritize developing a more comprehensive self-care routine

To Do:

After completing the assessment, identify the areas where you scored lowest and consider developing specific strategies to improve your self-care practices in those domains.

After completing this assessment, reflect on your results. Where are your strengths? Which areas need improvement? This assessment provides your "self-care baseline," a snapshot of where you are now and a guide for where to focus your efforts.

1. Setting Intentions for Your Self-Care Journey

Now that you have a clear picture of your current self-care practices, it's time to set intentions for your journey. Remember, effective goals are SMART: Specific, Measurable, Achievable, Relevant, and Time-bound.

For example, instead of a vague goal like "meditate more," a SMART goal would be "Practice mindfulness meditation for 10 minutes each morning for the next 30 days."

Consider your values as you set these goals. What matters most to you? How can your self-care practices align with and support these values? If connection is a core value, your self-care might include regular check-ins with loved ones or joining a community group.

Take a moment to envision your ideal self-care routine. What does your day look like when you're taking optimal care of yourself? Use this vision to inspire your goals and intentions.

1. Overcoming Common Self-Care Obstacles

As you begin your self-care journey, you may encounter some common obstacles. Let's address these head-on:

- Time constraints: Remember, self-care doesn't have to be time-consuming. Even five minutes of deep breathing or a quick gratitude practice can make a difference. Look for small pockets of time in your day that you can dedicate to self-care.
- Guilt or feelings of selfishness: Remind yourself that self-care isn't selfish—it's necessary. By taking care of yourself, you're better equipped to care for others and fulfill your responsibilities.
- Lack of consistency: Start small and build gradually. Consistency is more important than perfection. If you miss a day, simply start again the next day without self-judgment.

- Overwhelm: Focus on one or two areas of self-care at a time. As these become habitual, you can expand your practice.

1. **The Science of Habit Formation**

Understanding how habits form can help you create lasting change. Habits follow a loop: cue, routine, reward.

- Cue: The trigger that initiates the behavior
- Routine: The behavior itself
- Reward: The benefit you gain from the behavior

To create a new habit, identify a consistent cue (e.g., waking up in the morning), define the routine (e.g., five minutes of meditation), and recognize the reward (e.g., feeling calm and centered).

You can also use "habit stacking," where you attach a new habit to an existing one. For example, "After I pour my morning coffee (existing habit), I will write three things I'm grateful for (new habit)."

Remember, forming new habits takes time. Be patient with yourself and celebrate small victories along the way.

As we conclude this chapter, reflect on what you've learned about the foundations of self-care. In the coming chapters, we'll explore specific strategies and rituals to enhance your self-care practice, building on this foundation. Remember, self-care is a journey, not a destination. Each step you take is progress, no matter how small it may seem.

2

Chapter 2: Morning Rituals for a Positive Start

1. **The power of a consistent morning routine**

A consistent morning routine sets the tone for the entire day, influencing productivity, mood, and overall well-being. Research supports the importance of morning routines:

- A study published in the Journal of General Psychology (2019) found that individuals who followed a consistent morning routine reported lower levels of stress and higher levels of positive affect throughout the day (Kitsantas et al., 2019).
- Neuropsychologist Dr. Sanam Hafeez explains that routines help reduce anxiety by creating a sense of structure and familiarity, which is especially beneficial in the morning when cortisol levels are naturally higher (Hafeez, 2020).
- The book "The Miracle Morning" by Hal Elrod popularized the concept of transformative morning routines, suggesting that dedicating time to personal development activities in the morning can lead to

significant life improvements (Elrod, 2012).

Practical Application: Use the "Design Your Ideal Morning" worksheet below to plan your perfect morning routine:

Design Your Ideal Morning Worksheet

1. Wake-up Time: What time would you like to wake up? _________ AM
2. First Action: What's the first thing you want to do upon waking? (e.g., drink water, stretch) Action: _____________________________
   Duration: _________ minutes
3. Morning Rituals: List 3-5 activities you'd like to include in your morning routine: a. Activity: _____________________________
   Duration: _________ minutes b. Activity: _____________________________
   Duration: _________ minutes

c. Activity: _____________________________ Duration: _________ minutes

d. Activity: _____________________________ Duration: _________ minutes

e. Activity: _____________________________ Duration: _________ minutes

1. Nourishment: What would your ideal breakfast be? Breakfast: _____________________________ Time to prepare/eat: _________________ minutes
2. Preparation for the Day: What do you need to do to feel prepared for your day?

Action: _____________________________ Duration: _________ minutes

6. Ideal End Time: What time would you like your morning routine to

end?

__________________ AM

7. Total Duration: Calculate the total time for your ideal morning: _________ minutes

8. Top 3 Priorities: Which three morning activities are most important to you?

1 ____

2 ____

3 ____

9. Potential Obstacles: What might prevent you from following this routine?

____

____

10.Solutions: How can you overcome these obstacles?

____

____

11.Gradual Implementation: If this routine feels overwhelming, which one small

change can you start with tomorrow?

____

12.Commitment: I commit to trying this morning routine for _________ days.

Remember, the perfect morning routine is one that energizes you and sets a positive tone for your day. Be flexible and adjust as needed!

This worksheet allows you to thoughtfully plan your ideal morning routine while considering practical factors like time constraints and potential obstacles. It also encourages commitment and gradual implementation for sustainable change.

1. **Mindful wake-up practices**

Incorporating mindfulness into the wake-up process can significantly impact mental state and set a positive tone for the day:

- A study in the journal Mindfulness (2020) found that starting the day with a brief mindfulness practice led to increased positive affect and decreased negative affect throughout the day (Smeets et al., 2020).
- The concept of "sleep inertia," the groggy feeling upon waking, can be mitigated by gentle, mindful wake-up practices according to sleep researcher Dr. Allison Harvey (Harvey et al., 2016).

Mindful wake-up practices may include:

- Gentle stretching in bed
- Deep breathing exercises
- Gratitude reflection
- Body scan meditation

Practical Application: Use the following guide to track your consistency with mindful wake-up practices and note changes in mood and energy levels:

Mindful Morning Checklist

Week of: _______________________

Instructions: Check off each practice you complete daily. Rate your mood and energy

levels on a scale of 1–10 (1 = lowest, 10 = highest) after your morning routine.

Mindful Practice Mon Tue Wed Thu Fri Sat Sun

> **Gentle Stretching**
>
> **Deep Breathing**
>
> **Body Scan**
>
> **Gratitude Reflection**
>
> **Mindful Breakfast**
>
> **Nature Observation**
>
> **Journaling**

Daily Reflection:

Mood (1-10) Energy (1-10) Notes on how you feel

> **Monday**
>
> **Tuesday**
>
> **Wednesday**
>
> **Thursday**
>
> **Friday**
>
> **Saturday**
>
> **Sunday**

Weekly Reflection:

1. Which mindful practices did you find most beneficial this week?
2. Did you notice any patterns in your mood or energy levels?
3. What challenges did you face in maintaining your mindful morning routine?
4. How can you address these challenges next week?
5. What positive changes have you noticed since starting this mindful morning routine?
6. Set an intention for next week's mindful mornings:

Remember, consistency is key. Even small, regular practices can lead to significant improvements in your overall well-being.

This worksheet allows you to track your daily mindful practices, monitor changes in mood and energy levels, and reflect on your progress over the week. It encourages consistency while also promoting self-reflection and continuous improvement of your mindful morning routine.

1. **Nutritious breakfast ideas for brain health**

A nutritious breakfast is crucial for cognitive function and overall brain health:

- Research published in the journal Nutrients (2021) indicates that a breakfast rich in protein and complex carbohydrates can improve cognitive performance and mood throughout the morning (Galioto & Spitznagel, 2021).
- The Brain Health Kitchen by Dr. Annie Fenn emphasizes the importance of including brain-boosting foods like berries, nuts, and omega-3 rich fish in breakfast meals (Fenn, 2022).

Nutritious breakfast ideas:

- Greek yogurt with berries and walnuts
- Whole grain toast with avocado and eggs
- Overnight oats with chia seeds and fruit
- Spinach and mushroom omelet

Practical Application: Develop a week-long meal plan of brain-healthy breakfasts.

Here's a "Brain Food Breakfast Builder" worksheet you can mix and match brain-healthy ingredients to create nutritious breakfast combinations:

Brain Food Breakfast Builder

Instructions: Choose one item from each category to create your brain-boosting breakfast. Aim for a combination of protein, complex carbohydrates, healthy fats, and antioxidants.

1. Protein (Choose 1-2): ☐ Greek yogurt ☐ Eggs ☐ Smoked salmon ☐ Tofu ☐ Lean turkey ☐ Cottage cheese ☐ Nut butter (almond, peanut, cashew)
2. Complex Carbohydrates (Choose 1): ☐ Whole grain bread ☐ Oatmeal ☐ Quinoa ☐ Brown rice ☐ Sweet potato ☐ Whole grain cereal ☐ Buckwheat pancakes
3. Fruits (Choose 1-2): ☐ Blueberries ☐ Strawberries ☐ Banana ☐ Apple ☐ Oranges ☐ Blackberries ☐ Kiwi
4. Vegetables (Choose 1-2): ☐ Spinach ☐ Kale ☐ Tomatoes ☐ Avocado ☐ Bell peppers ☐ Mushrooms ☐ Broccoli
5. Nuts and Seeds (Choose 1): ☐ Walnuts ☐ Almonds ☐ Pumpkin seeds ☐ Chia seeds ☐ Flaxseeds ☐ Sunflower seeds ☐ Hemp seeds
6. Healthy Fats (Choose 1): ☐ Olive oil ☐ Coconut oil ☐ Avocado ☐ Grass-fed butter ☐ MCT oil
7. Extras (Optional): ☐ Cinnamon ☐ Turmeric ☐ Dark chocolate chips ☐ Honey ☐ Maple syrup ☐ Green tea ☐ Coffee

My Brain-Boosting Breakfast Combination:

Protein: ____

Complex Carb: ____

Fruit(s): ____

Vegetable(s): ____

Nuts/Seeds: ____

Healthy Fat: ____

Extra: ____

Preparation method (e.g., smoothie, bowl, sandwich):

____

Now, create 3 different brain-healthy breakfast combinations for the week:

1. ____

2. ____

3. ____

Remember: A brain-healthy breakfast should include a mix of nutrients to support cognitive function, provide sustained energy, and promote overall well-being. Experiment with different combinations to find what works best for you!

This worksheet allows you to create customized, brain-healthy breakfast combinations by choosing from a variety of nutritious ingredients. It encourages creativity while ensuring a balance of essential nutrients for optimal brain function.

1. **Morning movement: Yoga, stretching, or light exercise**

Incorporating movement into the morning routine can have significant benefits for both physical and mental health:

- A study in the British Journal of Sports Medicine (2019) found that morning exercise improved attention, visual learning, and decision-making throughout the day (Wheeler et al., 2019).

- Yoga, in particular, has been shown to reduce morning cortisol levels and improve overall stress response, according to research published in the Journal of Alternative and Complementary Medicine (Thirthalli et al., 2013).

Morning movement options:

- 10-minute yoga flow
- Gentle stretching routine
- Brisk walk around the neighborhood
- Light bodyweight exercises (squats, push-ups, lunges)

Practical Application: Here's a "Morning Movement Tracker" work-sheet where you can log their daily morning movement:

Morning Movement Tracker

Week of: _______________________

Instructions: Use this tracker to log your morning movement activities. Note the type
of exercise, duration, and how you feel afterward. Rate your energy and mood on a
scale of 1–10 (1 = lowest, 10 = highest) after your morning movement.

Weekly Reflection:

1. Which morning movement did you enjoy the most this week?
2. Did you notice any patterns in your energy or mood levels related to your morning movement?

3. What challenges did you face in maintaining your morning movement routine?

4. How can you address these challenges next week?

5. What positive changes have you noticed since starting your morning movement routine?

6. Set a movement goal for next week:

Morning Movement Ideas:

☐ Yoga flow ☐ Stretching routine ☐ Brisk Walk ☐ Light jog ☐ Bodyweight exercises

(squats, pushups, lunges) ☐ Dance ☐ Tai Chi ☐ Pilates ☐ Cycling ☐ Swimming ☐ Jump

rope ☐ HighIntensity Interval Training (HIIT)

Remember: The best morning movement is one that you enjoy and can consistently

maintain. Even a few minutes of movement can set a positive tone for your day!

This worksheet allows you to track their daily morning movement activities, monitor

changes in energy and mood levels, and reflect on your progress over the week. It

encourages consistency while also promoting selfreflection and goalsetting for your

morning movement routine.

3

Chapter 3: Daytime Rituals for Stress Management

1. **Micro-breaks and their impact on productivity and mental health**

Micro-breaks are short, voluntary pauses taken throughout the workday to help refresh and refocus the mind. These brief interludes, typically lasting between 30 seconds to 5 minutes, can significantly impact both productivity and mental health.

Research has shown that regular micro-breaks can lead to increased productivity and improved mental well-being. A study published in the Journal of Applied Psychology found that employees who took short breaks throughout the day reported higher levels of engagement and lower levels of fatigue compared to those who didn't (Kim et al., 2018).

Micro-breaks work by allowing the brain to momentarily disengage from focused tasks, reducing cognitive fatigue and improving attention span. Dr. Alejandro Lleras, a psychology professor at the University of Illinois, explains: "From a practical standpoint, our research suggests that, when faced with long tasks, it is best to impose brief breaks on yourself. Brief mental breaks will actually help you stay focused on your task" (University of Illinois at Urbana-Champaign, 2011).

Some effective micro-break activities include:

- Standing up and stretching
- Taking a short walk
- Practicing deep breathing exercises
- Looking at nature or out a window
- Engaging in a brief mindfulness exercise

To implement micro-breaks effectively, consider using the Pomodoro Technique, which involves working for 25-minute intervals followed by 5-minute breaks. This structured approach can help maintain focus while ensuring regular periods of rest.

1. **Mindfulness practices for the workplace**

Mindfulness, the practice of being fully present and engaged in the current moment, has gained significant traction in workplace wellness programs due to its proven benefits for stress reduction and improved focus.

A meta-analysis published in the Journal of Occupational Health Psychology found that mindfulness-based interventions in the workplace led to significant improvements in employee well-being, including reduced stress, anxiety, and burnout (Lomas et al., 2017).

Here are some mindfulness practices that can be easily incorporated into the workplace:

a) Mindful breathing: Take a few minutes to focus on your breath, noticing the sensation of inhaling and exhaling. This simple practice can help center your thoughts and reduce stress.

b) Body scan: Spend a few moments systematically focusing on different parts of your body, noting any tension or discomfort. This practice can improve body awareness and promote relaxation.

c) Mindful listening: During meetings or conversations, practice giving your full attention to the speaker, without planning your response or allowing your mind to wander.

d) Mindful transitions: Use the time between tasks or meetings to practice mindfulness. Take a few deep breaths and set an intention for your next activity.

e) Mindful eating: During lunch or snack breaks, pay full attention to the experience of eating, noticing flavors, textures, and sensations.

Dr. Ellen Langer, a Harvard psychology professor and mindfulness expert, emphasizes the importance of mindfulness in the workplace: "When people are mindful, they're more innovative and more productive. They make better decisions. They're more charismatic. They have more energy" (Langer, 2014).

1. The art of saying "no" and setting boundaries

Learning to say "no" and set healthy boundaries is crucial for managing stress and maintaining work-life balance. However, many people struggle with this skill due to fear of conflict or a desire to please others.

According to Dr. Brené Brown, a research professor at the University of Houston, "Daring to set boundaries is about having the courage to love ourselves even when we risk disappointing others" (Brown, 2010).

Here are some strategies for effectively saying "no" and setting boundaries:

a) Prioritize your commitments: Clearly define your priorities and evaluate new requests against them.

b) Use "I" statements: Frame your refusal in terms of your needs and limitations, rather than criticizing the request.

c) Offer alternatives: If possible, suggest other solutions or people who might be able to help.

d) Practice empathy: Acknowledge the other person's needs while still maintaining your boundary.

e) Be clear and concise: Avoid over-explaining or apologizing excessively for your decision.

Research published in the Journal of Occupational and Environmental Medicine found that employees who maintained clear work-life boundaries reported lower levels of stress and higher job satisfaction (Kossek et al., 2012).

1. Lunchtime rituals for refueling body and mind

Lunchtime offers a valuable opportunity to recharge both physically and mentally. Developing intentional lunchtime rituals can significantly impact your afternoon productivity and overall well-being.

Here are some evidence-based lunchtime rituals to consider:

a) Mindful eating: As mentioned earlier, practicing mindful eating during lunch can enhance digestion and satisfaction. A study in the American Journal of Clinical Nutrition found that mindful eating led to greater feelings of fullness and reduced calorie intake (Arch et al., 2016).

b) Social connection: Sharing lunch with colleagues or friends can boost mood and reduce stress. Research published in PLOS ONE showed that social connection during breaks at work led to improved well-being and job performance (Kim et al., 2017).

c) Physical activity: A short walk or light exercise during lunch can improve cognitive function and mood. A study in the Scandinavian Journal of Medicine & Science in Sports found that lunchtime walks improved enthusiasm, relaxation, and nervousness at work (Thøgersen-

Ntoumani et al., 2015).

d) Nature exposure: Spending time in nature, even briefly, can reduce stress and improve cognitive function. Research in the International Journal of Environmental Research and Public Health found that as little as 10 minutes in a natural setting can have significant psychological benefits (Hunter et al., 2019).

e) Power napping: A short nap (10-20 minutes) can improve alertness and performance. However, it's important to keep naps brief to avoid sleep inertia, as noted in a study published in Sleep (Lovato & Lack, 2010).

Dr. Sabine Sonnentag, a professor of work and organizational psychology at the University of Mannheim, emphasizes the importance of lunchtime recovery: "Taking time to relax and detach from work during lunch breaks can help employees feel more vigorous and less fatigued when they return to work" (Sonnentag et al., 2017).

By incorporating these daytime rituals into your routine, you can effectively manage stress, improve productivity, and enhance overall well-being. Remember that consistency is key, and it may take time to find the practices that work best for you.

4

Chapter 4: Evening Rituals for Restful Sleep

1. **The importance of sleep for mental health**

Sleep is a fundamental pillar of mental health, playing a crucial role in cognitive function, emotional regulation, and overall psychological well-being. The relationship between sleep and mental health is bidirectional – poor sleep can exacerbate mental health issues, while mental health problems can disrupt sleep patterns.

Dr. Matthew Walker, Professor of Neuroscience and Psychology at the University of California, Berkeley, emphasizes: "Sleep is the single most effective thing we can do to reset our brain and body health each day" (Walker, 2017).

Key aspects of sleep's impact on mental health include:

a) Emotional regulation: Sleep helps process emotional experiences and regulate mood. A study published in Current Biology found that sleep deprivation amplifies neural reactivity to negative stimuli while impairing the brain's ability to regulate emotions (Yoo et al., 2007).

b) Cognitive function: Adequate sleep is essential for attention, learning, and memory consolidation. Research in the journal Sleep shows that even moderate sleep deprivation can impair cognitive performance to a degree equivalent to alcohol intoxication (Williamson & Feyer, 2000).

c) Stress resilience: Quality sleep enhances the body's ability to cope with stress. A study in the journal Sleep Medicine Reviews found that sleep loss alters the functioning of the hypothalamic-pituitary-adrenal (HPA) axis, which regulates the stress response (Meerlo et al., 2008).

d) Mental health disorders: Chronic sleep problems are strongly associated with increased risk of developing mental health disorders. A meta-analysis published in BMC Psychiatry revealed that insomnia significantly increases the risk of depression, anxiety, and substance abuse (Hertenstein et al., 2019).

The National Sleep Foundation recommends 7-9 hours of sleep per night for adults. However, it's not just quantity but also quality of sleep that matters. Implementing effective evening rituals can significantly improve both sleep duration and quality.

1. Creating a wind-down routine

A consistent wind-down routine signals to your body and mind that it's time to transition from the activities of the day to restful sleep. This routine helps regulate your circadian rhythm and promotes the production of sleep-inducing hormones like melatonin.

Dr. Phyllis Zee, Chief of Sleep Medicine at Northwestern University, states: "The hour before bed is gold. It's a time to have a routine that's relaxing and sleep-promoting" (Northwestern Medicine, 2021).

Components of an effective wind-down routine may include:

a) Consistent timing: Start your routine at the same time each night, ideally 60-90 minutes before your intended bedtime.

b) Digital sunset: Reduce exposure to blue light from electronic devices, which can suppress melatonin production. A study in the Journal of Applied Physiology found that exposure to blue light in the evening can delay the onset of REM sleep (Chellappa et al., 2013).

c) Relaxing activities: Engage in calming activities such as reading, gentle stretching, or listening to soothing music. A meta-analysis published in the Journal of Music Therapy found that music can significantly improve sleep quality in adults with insomnia (Wang et al., 2014).

d) Aromatherapy: Certain scents, like lavender, have been shown to promote relaxation and improve sleep quality. A study in the Journal of Alternative and Complementary Medicine found that lavender aromatherapy improved sleep quality in college students (Lillehei et al., 2015).

e) Journaling: Writing down thoughts or creating a to-do list for the next day can help clear the mind. Research in the Journal of Experimental Psychology found that writing a to-do list before bed helped people fall asleep faster (Scullin et al., 2018).

f) Light snack: If hungry, opt for a light, sleep-promoting snack rich in tryptophan, magnesium, or complex carbohydrates. A small study in the Journal of Psychiatric Research found that consuming kiwifruit before bed improved sleep onset, duration, and efficiency (Lin et al., 2011).

1. **Bedroom environment optimization**

Your sleep environment plays a crucial role in the quality of your rest. Optimizing your bedroom can significantly improve sleep onset and maintenance.

Key factors to consider in bedroom optimization include:

a) Temperature: Maintain a cool room temperature, ideally between 60-67°F (15-19°C). Dr. Christopher Winter, Medical Director of the

Martha Jefferson Hospital Sleep Medicine Center, explains: "Temperature is an important factor in getting a good night's sleep. Typically, it's thought that a cool room around 65 degrees Fahrenheit is best for sleep" (Sleep.org, 2021).

b) Darkness: Ensure your bedroom is as dark as possible. Use blackout curtains or an eye mask if necessary. A study in the Journal of Pineal Research found that even dim light exposure during sleep can suppress melatonin production and potentially impact health (Obayashi et al., 2013).

c) Noise control: Minimize disruptive noises. If complete silence isn't possible, consider using a white noise machine or earplugs. Research in Sleep Medicine found that continuous white noise can help people fall asleep faster (Messineo et al., 2017).

d) Comfortable bedding: Invest in a supportive mattress and pillows. A study in Applied Ergonomics showed that new bedding systems increased sleep quality and reduced back discomfort (Jacobson et al., 2008).

e) Air quality: Ensure good ventilation and consider using an air purifier. Research in the journal Indoor Air found that better air quality was associated with improved sleep quality (Mishra et al., 2018).

f) Clutter-free space: Keep your bedroom tidy and organized. A study in the journal Sleep found that people who sleep in cluttered rooms are more likely to have sleep problems (Roster et al., 2016).

1. **Relaxation techniques for better sleep**

Incorporating relaxation techniques into your evening routine can help calm the mind and prepare the body for sleep. These practices can be particularly beneficial for those struggling with racing thoughts or anxiety at bedtime.

Effective relaxation techniques include:

a) Progressive Muscle Relaxation (PMR): This involves tensing and then relaxing different muscle groups in sequence. A meta-analysis in Sleep Medicine Reviews found that PMR significantly improved sleep quality (Neuendorf et al., 2015).

b) Deep breathing exercises: Techniques like 4-7-8 breathing (inhale for 4 counts, hold for 7, exhale for 8) can activate the parasympathetic nervous system, promoting relaxation. Dr. Andrew Weil, founder of the University of Arizona Center for Integrative Medicine, recommends this technique as a "natural tranquilizer for the nervous system" (Weil, 2016).

c) Mindfulness meditation: Focusing on the present moment can help quiet a busy mind. A study in JAMA Internal Medicine found that mindfulness meditation improved sleep quality in older adults with sleep disturbances (Black et al., 2015).

d) Guided imagery: Visualizing peaceful, calming scenes can promote relaxation. Research in the Journal of Advanced Nursing showed that guided imagery significantly improved sleep quality in cancer patients (Chen et al., 2018).

e) Yoga Nidra: This guided meditation practice has been shown to improve sleep quality. A study in the Indian Journal of Medical Research found that practicing Yoga Nidra improved sleep quality in college professors (Rani et al., 2012).

f) Biofeedback: Using devices to monitor physiological processes can help individuals learn to control these processes for better relaxation. A review in Sleep Medicine Clinics found that biofeedback interventions can be effective for treating insomnia (Lovato et al., 2019).

Dr. Sat Bir Singh Khalsa, Assistant Professor of Medicine at Harvard Medical School, emphasizes the importance of these techniques: "Relaxation practices are powerful tools for calming the mind and body, making the transition into sleep easier and more natural" (Khalsa, 2012).

By understanding the importance of sleep for mental health and implementing these evening rituals – including a consistent wind-down routine, optimized sleep environment, and effective relaxation techniques – you can significantly improve your sleep quality and overall well-being. Remember that developing new habits takes time, so be patient and consistent in your approach to cultivating better sleep practices.

5

Chapter 5: Emotional Self-Care Rituals

1. **Journaling for emotional processing**

Journaling is a powerful tool for emotional processing and self-reflection. It provides a safe, private space to explore thoughts and feelings, helping individuals gain clarity and insight into their emotional experiences.

Dr. James Pennebaker, a pioneer in the research of expressive writing, states: "When people are given the opportunity to write about emotional upheavals, they often experience improved health. They go to the doctor less. They have changes in immune function" (Pennebaker, 1997).

Key benefits of journaling for emotional processing include:

a) Stress reduction: A study published in the Journal of Experimental Psychology found that expressive writing reduced intrusive and avoidant thoughts about negative events and improved working memory (Klein & Boals, 2001).

b) Emotional clarity: Journaling helps identify and name emotions, a process known as affect labeling. Research in the journal Psychological Science showed that labeling emotions reduces their intensity (Lieber-

32

man et al., 2007).

c) Problem-solving: Writing about problems can lead to new insights and solutions. A study in the Journal of Personality and Social Psychology found that writing about life goals was associated with higher academic performance (Pennebaker & Francis, 1996).

d) Emotional regulation: Regular journaling can improve emotional regulation skills. A meta-analysis published in the Clinical Psychology Review found that expressive writing interventions resulted in improved psychological health (Frattaroli, 2006).

Effective journaling techniques include:

- Stream of consciousness writing
- Structured prompts (e.g., "Today I felt...")
- Gratitude journaling
- Reflective journaling (analyzing past experiences)

Dr. Kristin Neff, an expert in self-compassion, recommends: "Try keeping a self-compassion journal for one week (or longer if you like). Journaling is an effective way to express emotions, and has been found to enhance both mental and physical well-being" (Neff, 2011).

1. **Practicing gratitude and its effects on the brain**

Gratitude practice is a powerful emotional self-care ritual that has been shown to have significant positive effects on mental health and brain function.

Dr. Robert Emmons, a leading gratitude researcher, defines gratitude as "an affirmation of goodness in one's life and the recognition that the sources of this goodness lie at least partially outside the self" (Emmons & McCullough, 2003).

The neurological effects of gratitude include:

a) Increased dopamine and serotonin production: These neurotransmitters are associated with feelings of happiness and well-being. A study in NeuroImage found that gratitude practice activated brain regions associated with the neurotransmitter dopamine (Kini et al., 2016).

b) Improved neural modulation of the prefrontal cortex: This area is associated with positive emotions. Research published in Frontiers in Psychology showed that gratitude interventions led to increased activity in the medial prefrontal cortex (Kini et al., 2016).

c) Enhanced activity in the anterior cingulate cortex: This region is involved in emotional regulation. A study in NeuroImage found that writing gratitude letters increased activity in this area (Kini et al., 2016).

d) Structural changes in the brain: Long-term gratitude practice has been associated with increased grey matter volume in the right inferior temporal gyrus, as shown in a study published in Scientific Reports (Cheng et al., 2022).

Practical gratitude exercises include:

- Keeping a daily gratitude journal
- Writing gratitude letters
- Practicing mindful appreciation of daily experiences
- Gratitude meditation

Dr. Alex Korb, neuroscientist and author, notes: "Gratitude can have such a powerful impact on your life because it engages your brain in a virtuous cycle. Your brain only has so much power to focus its attention. It cannot easily focus on both positive and negative stimuli" (Korb, 2015).

1. **Self-compassion exercises**

Self-compassion involves treating oneself with kindness and understanding, particularly in times of failure or difficulty. It's a crucial aspect of emotional self-care that can significantly improve mental well-being.

Dr. Kristin Neff, a pioneer in self-compassion research, defines it as having three components: self-kindness, common humanity, and mindfulness (Neff, 2003).

Benefits of self-compassion include:

a) Reduced anxiety and depression: A meta-analysis published in Mindfulness found that self-compassion interventions were associated with reduced symptoms of anxiety and depression (Wilson et al., 2019).

b) Improved emotional resilience: Research in the Journal of Personality shows that self-compassionate individuals demonstrate greater emotional resilience in the face of negative events (Leary et al., 2007).

c) Enhanced motivation: Contrary to popular belief, self-compassion doesn't lead to complacency. A study in Personality and Social Psychology Bulletin found that self-compassion was associated with greater personal improvement motivation (Breines & Chen, 2012).

d) Better body image: A meta-analysis in Body Image revealed that self-compassion interventions led to improvements in body image and eating behaviors (Turk & Waller, 2020).

Effective self-compassion exercises include:

- Self-compassionate letter writing: Write a letter to yourself from the perspective of a compassionate friend.
- Loving-kindness meditation: Practice directing feelings of love and kindness towards yourself and others.
- Self-compassion break: In moments of difficulty, acknowledge your pain, remind yourself of common humanity, and offer yourself kindness.
- Changing critical self-talk: Learn to recognize and reframe self-critical thoughts in a more compassionate way.

Dr. Christopher Germer, a clinical psychologist and mindfulness expert, states: "Self-compassion is simply giving the same kindness to ourselves that we would give to others" (Germer, 2009).

1. Emotional release techniques (e.g., art therapy, music)

Emotional release techniques provide healthy outlets for expressing and processing emotions. These methods can be particularly beneficial for individuals who struggle with verbalizing their feelings.

Art therapy: Art therapy uses creative processes to improve mental health and well-being. A systematic review published in Frontiers in Psychology found that art therapy interventions were effective in reducing depression and anxiety symptoms (Abbing et al., 2018).

Benefits of art therapy include:

- Stress reduction
- Improved emotional expression
- Enhanced self-awareness
- Increased sense of control

Dr. Cathy Malchiodi, an expert in art therapy, explains: "Art therapy is a way to gain insight into emotions, thoughts, and feelings that might otherwise remain hidden or difficult to express verbally" (Malchiodi, 2011).

Music therapy: Music therapy involves using music to address physical, emotional, and social needs. A meta-analysis in the Journal of Music Therapy found that music interventions had significant effects on reducing anxiety and improving mood in various populations (Pelletier, 2004).

Benefits of music therapy include:

- Emotion regulation
- Stress reduction
- Improved mood
- Enhanced cognitive function

Dr. Joke Bradt, a music therapy researcher, notes: "Active music engagement allows for opportunities to practice problem-solving and coping skills within the safety of a therapeutic environment" (Bradt et al., 2015).

Other emotional release techniques:

- Dance/movement therapy
- Drama therapy
- Expressive writing
- Somatic experiencing

Dr. Peter Levine, developer of Somatic Experiencing, states: "Trauma is a fact of life. It does not, however, have to be a life sentence. Not only can trauma be healed, but with appropriate guidance and support, it can be transformative" (Levine, 2010).

Incorporating these emotional self-care rituals into daily life can significantly enhance emotional well-being and resilience. It's important to remember that different techniques may work better for different individuals, and it may take time to find the most effective combination of practices.

6

Chapter 6: Physical Self-Care Rituals

1. **Exercise as a tool for mental health**

Exercise is not just beneficial for physical health; it's also a powerful tool for maintaining and improving mental health. Regular physical activity has been shown to have significant positive effects on mood, cognitive function, and overall mental well-being.

Dr. John Ratey, Associate Clinical Professor of Psychiatry at Harvard Medical School, states: "Exercise is the single most powerful tool you have to optimize your brain function" (Ratey, 2008).

Key mental health benefits of exercise include:

a) Reduced symptoms of depression and anxiety: A meta-analysis published in JAMA Psychiatry found that physical activity was significantly associated with reduced odds of depression (Schuch et al., 2018). Another study in Frontiers in Psychiatry showed that exercise interventions were effective in reducing anxiety symptoms (Stubbs et al., 2017).

b) Improved cognitive function: Research in the British Journal of Sports Medicine demonstrated that regular aerobic exercise increases the size of the hippocampus, leading to improved memory and cognitive function (Firth et al., 2018).

c) Stress reduction: Exercise helps reduce levels of stress hormones like cortisol and adrenaline. A study in Psych neuroendocrinology found that regular exercisers had lower cortisol responses to psychological stress (Zschucke et al., 2015).

d) Enhanced self-esteem: Physical activity has been linked to improved self-esteem and body image. A meta-analysis in Psychology of Sport and Exercise found a significant positive effect of exercise on self-esteem (Spence et al., 2005).

e) Better sleep: Regular exercise can improve sleep quality, which is crucial for mental health. Research in the journal Sleep Medicine found that exercise was associated with improved sleep quality and duration (Kredlow et al., 2015).

Effective exercise strategies for mental health:

- Aim for at least 150 minutes of moderate-intensity or 75 minutes of vigorous-intensity aerobic activity per week, as recommended by the World Health Organization.
- Include both aerobic exercises (e.g., walking, jogging, cycling) and strength training in your routine.
- Consider mind-body exercises like yoga or tai chi, which have been shown to have additional mental health benefits.
- Find activities you enjoy to increase adherence and motivation.

Dr. Wendy Suzuki, Professor of Neural Science and Psychology at New York University, emphasizes: "Exercise is the most transformative thing you can do for your brain today" (Suzuki, 2017).

1. The mental health benefits of proper nutrition

Nutrition plays a crucial role in mental health, influencing mood, cognitive function, and overall psychological well-being. A growing body of research supports the connection between diet and mental health, leading to the emergence of the field of nutritional psychiatry.

Dr. Drew Ramsey, Assistant Clinical Professor of Psychiatry at Columbia University, states: "The emerging field of nutritional psychiatry is finding that the food you eat directly affects the structure of your digestive tract, the function of your brain, and, ultimately, your mood" (Ramsey, 2016).

Key aspects of nutrition's impact on mental health include:

a) Brain function: Certain nutrients are essential for optimal brain function. For example, omega-3 fatty acids, found in fish and flaxseeds, are crucial for brain health. A meta-analysis in the Journal of Clinical Psychiatry found that omega-3 supplementation was effective in reducing symptoms of depression (Grosso et al., 2016).

b) Gut-brain axis: The gut microbiome plays a significant role in mental health through the gut-brain axis. A review in Clinical Psychopharmacology and Neuroscience highlighted the role of probiotics in reducing symptoms of depression and anxiety (Wallace & Milev, 2017).

c) Blood sugar regulation: Stable blood sugar levels are important for mood regulation. A study in the American Journal of Clinical Nutrition found that a diet with a high glycemic load was associated with increased risk of depression (Gangwisch et al., 2015).

d) Inflammation: Chronic inflammation has been linked to mental health disorders. An anti-inflammatory diet rich in fruits, vegetables, and omega-3 fatty acids may help reduce the risk of depression. Research in Brain, Behavior, and Immunity found that a Mediterranean-style diet was associated with reduced risk of depression (Lassale et al., 2019).

Nutritional strategies for mental health:

- Incorporate more whole foods, including fruits, vegetables, whole grains, and lean proteins.
- Increase intake of omega-3 fatty acids through fish, flaxseeds, or supplements.
- Include fermented foods like yogurt, kefir, and sauerkraut to support gut health.
- Reduce consumption of processed foods, added sugars, and unhealthy fats.

Dr. Felice Jacka, Director of the Food and Mood Centre at Deakin University, emphasizes: "A healthy diet is protective and an unhealthy diet is a risk factor for depression and anxiety" (Jacka et al., 2017).

1. **Hydration and its impact on mood**

Proper hydration is often overlooked in discussions of mental health, but it plays a crucial role in cognitive function, mood regulation, and overall psychological well-being. Even mild dehydration can have significant effects on mental state and performance.

Dr. Harris Lieberman, a research psychologist at the U.S. Army Research Institute of Environmental Medicine, notes: "Dehydration affects all people, and staying properly hydrated is just as important for those who work all day at a computer as it is for marathon runners" (Lieberman, 2007).

Key aspects of hydration's impact on mental health include:

a) Cognitive function: Mild dehydration can impair various aspects of brain function. A study published in the British Journal of Nutrition found that even mild dehydration was associated with decreased cognitive performance, particularly for tasks requiring attention, executive function, and coordination (Masento et al., 2014).

b) Mood regulation: Dehydration can negatively affect mood. Research in the Journal of Nutrition found that mild dehydration was associated with degraded mood, increased perception of task difficulty, lower concentration, and headache symptoms (Armstrong et al., 2012).

c) Fatigue and energy levels: Proper hydration is crucial for maintaining energy levels. A study in Physiology & Behavior demonstrated that dehydration increased fatigue, reduced motivation, and made tasks seem more difficult (Pross et al., 2013).

d) Stress response: Dehydration can increase cortisol levels, the body's stress hormone. Research in Psych neuroendocrinology showed that inadequate hydration was associated with higher cortisol levels and increased perceived stress (Pross et al., 2014).

Strategies for maintaining proper hydration:

- Aim to drink at least 8 glasses (64 ounces) of water per day, adjusting for activity level and climate.
- Keep a water bottle visible and easily accessible throughout the day.
- Set reminders to drink water regularly.
- Consume water-rich foods like fruits and vegetables.
- Monitor urine color as an indicator of hydration status (pale yellow indicates good hydration).

Dr. Joshua Gowin, a neuroscientist, emphasizes: "When you're properly hydrated, your brain works optimally. It's easier to concentrate, and you're more alert. You'll also experience better memory function" (Gowin, 2018).

1. **The importance of regular health check-ups**

Regular health check-ups are a crucial component of physical self-care that can have significant implications for mental health. These preventive visits allow for early detection and management of health issues, which can prevent or mitigate associated mental health challenges.

Dr. Michael Kidd, Professor of Primary Care Reform at the University of Toronto, states: "Regular health checks are an important part of preventive health care. They can help find problems early or before they start" (Kidd, 2015).

Key aspects of the importance of regular health check-ups include:

a) Early detection of health issues: Regular check-ups can identify health problems before they become serious. A study in the American Journal of Managed Care found that preventive care was associated with reduced hospitalizations for chronic conditions (Goetzel et al., 2005).

b) Management of chronic conditions: For those with chronic health conditions, regular check-ups are crucial for ongoing management. Research in the Journal of General Internal Medicine showed that regular primary care visits were associated with better management of chronic diseases and reduced mortality (Levine et al., 2019).

c) Mental health screening: Many primary care providers include mental health screenings in regular check-ups. A study in the Journal of General Internal Medicine found that screening for depression in primary care settings led to improved outcomes (O'Connor et al., 2009).

d) Stress reduction: Knowing that you're taking care of your health can reduce anxiety about potential health issues. A survey by the American Psychological Association found that 65% of adults felt less stressed after visiting their healthcare provider (APA, 2019).

e) Lifestyle advice: Regular check-ups provide opportunities for healthcare providers to offer personalized advice on diet, exercise, and other lifestyle factors that impact both physical and mental health.

Recommended frequency of health check-ups:

· For adults aged 18-39: Every 2-3 years

- For adults aged 40-64: Every 1-2 years
- For adults 65 and older: Annually

These are general guidelines, and individuals with specific health concerns or risk factors may need more frequent check-ups.

Dr. Ranit Mishori, Professor of Family Medicine at Georgetown University School of Medicine, emphasizes: "Regular check-ups are an investment in your health. They give you a chance to talk to your doctor about any health concerns and get the screenings you need" (Mishori, 2015).

Incorporating these physical self-care rituals – regular exercise, proper nutrition, adequate hydration, and routine health check-ups – into daily life can significantly enhance both physical and mental well-being. It's important to remember that these practices work synergistically, and adopting a holistic approach to physical self-care can lead to the best outcomes for overall health and wellness.

7

Chapter 7: Social Self-Care Rituals

1. Nurturing relationships as a form of self-care

Nurturing relationships is a crucial aspect of social self-care that significantly impacts mental health and overall well-being. Positive social connections provide emotional support, reduce stress, and contribute to a sense of belonging and purpose.

Dr. Robert Waldinger, director of the Harvard Study of Adult Development, states: "The surprising finding is that our relationships and how happy we are in our relationships has a powerful influence on our health. Taking care of your body is important, but tending to your relationships is a form of self-care too" (Waldinger, 2015).

Key aspects of nurturing relationships include:

a) Improved mental health: Strong social connections are associated with better mental health outcomes. A meta-analysis published in PLOS Medicine found that individuals with stronger social relationships had a 50% increased likelihood of survival compared to those with weaker social relationships (Holt-Lunstad et al., 2010).

b) Stress reduction: Social support acts as a buffer against stress. Research in the journal Health Psychology showed that individuals with greater social support experienced lower cardiovascular reactivity to stress (Uchino et al., 1996).

c) Enhanced cognitive function: Engaging in social activities can help maintain cognitive function as we age. A study in the Journal of the International Neuropsychological Society found that higher levels of social engagement were associated with better cognitive function in older adults (Zunzunegui et al., 2003).

d) Increased longevity: Strong social connections are linked to increased longevity. The Harvard Study of Adult Development, which has followed participants for over 80 years, found that close relationships were better predictors of long and happy lives than social class, IQ, or even genes (Waldinger, 2015).

Strategies for nurturing relationships:

- Prioritize quality time with loved ones
- Practice active listening and empathy
- Express gratitude and appreciation regularly
- Engage in shared activities or hobbies
- Maintain regular communication, even if brief

Dr. Emma Seppälä, Science Director of Stanford University's Center for Compassion and Altruism Research and Education, emphasizes: "People who feel more connected to others have lower rates of anxiety and depression. Moreover, studies show they also have higher self-esteem, are more emphatic to others, more trusting and cooperative and, as a consequence, others are more open to trusting and cooperating with them" (Seppälä, 2014).

1. **Setting healthy boundaries in relationships**

Setting and maintaining healthy boundaries is a crucial social self-care ritual that promotes emotional well-being, reduces stress, and fosters more satisfying relationships. Boundaries are the limits we set with others to protect our physical and emotional well-being.

Dr. Henry Cloud, a clinical psychologist and author, defines boundaries as "a property line that defines where you end and someone else begins" (Cloud & Townsend, 1992).

Key aspects of setting healthy boundaries include:

a) Improved self-esteem: Clear boundaries help maintain a sense of self and boost self-esteem. A study in the Journal of Counseling Psychology found that individuals with well-defined personal boundaries reported higher levels of self-esteem and lower levels of depression (Hartmann & Millea, 1996).

b) Reduced stress and anxiety: Setting boundaries can reduce stress by preventing over commitment and emotional exhaustion. Research in the Journal of Occupational Health Psychology showed that employees who set clear work-life boundaries experienced less stress and greater job satisfaction (Kossek et al., 2012).

c) Enhanced relationships: Healthy boundaries promote mutual respect and understanding in relationships. A study in the Journal of Marital and Family Therapy found that couples who maintained healthy boundaries reported higher relationship satisfaction (Knapp et al., 2017).

d) Improved mental health: Clear boundaries can protect against burnout and compassion fatigue, particularly in helping professions. A meta-analysis in Professional Psychology: Research and Practice found that maintaining professional boundaries was associated with lower levels of burnout among mental health professionals (Lee et al., 2011).

Strategies for setting healthy boundaries:

- Identify your limits and communicate them clearly
- Use "I" statements when expressing boundaries (e.g., "I feel over-

whelmed when...")
- Learn to say no without guilt
- Respect others' boundaries as you would want yours respected
- Regularly reassess and adjust your boundaries as needed

Dr. Brené Brown, research professor at the University of Houston, emphasizes: "Daring to set boundaries is about having the courage to love ourselves even when we risk disappointing others" (Brown, 2010).

1. The power of community and support groups

Engaging with community and support groups is a powerful social self-care ritual that can provide numerous benefits for mental health and overall well-being. These groups offer a sense of belonging, shared experiences, and collective support that can be particularly valuable during challenging times.

Dr. Irvin Yalom, professor emeritus of psychiatry at Stanford University, states: "The group, however, meets a deep human need to belong, to be part of a larger whole, to overcome isolation and alienation" (Yalom, 1995).

Key aspects of community and support groups include:

a) Improved mental health outcomes: Participation in support groups has been associated with improved mental health. A meta-analysis published in the American Journal of Community Psychology found that support group participation was associated with reduced symptoms of depression and anxiety (Pfeiffer et al., 2011).

b) Increased social support: Support groups provide a network of individuals who can offer emotional and practical support. Research in Social Science & Medicine showed that participation in community groups was associated with increased perceived social support and improved quality of life (Haslam et al., 2016).

c) Shared experiences and coping strategies: Support groups allow individuals to share experiences and learn from others facing similar challenges. A study in the Journal of Psychosocial Oncology found that cancer support groups helped participants develop more effective coping strategies (Ussher et al., 2006).

d) Reduced stigma: For individuals dealing with mental health issues or other stigmatized conditions, support groups can help reduce feelings of isolation and shame. Research in Psychiatric Services demonstrated that participation in peer support groups was associated with reduced self-stigma among individuals with mental illness (Corrigan et al., 2013).

Types of community and support groups:

- Mental health support groups (e.g., depression, anxiety)
- Chronic illness support groups
- Addiction recovery groups
- Grief support groups
- Professional or career-focused groups
- Hobby or interest-based communities

Dr. Kenneth Pargament, professor emeritus of psychology at Bowling Green State University, notes: "One of the most powerful ways to find meaning in difficult times is through connections with others who are facing similar struggles" (Pargament, 2007).

1. **Balancing solitude and social interaction**

Finding the right balance between solitude and social interaction is a crucial aspect of social self-care. While social connections are vital for mental health, periods of solitude are equally important for self-reflection, creativity, and emotional regulation.

Dr. Thuy-vy Nguyen, a researcher in solitude at the University of

Durham, states: "Solitude can be restorative and a powerful way to regulate our emotions. It can be refreshing and help us discover a sense of self" (Nguyen et al., 2018).

Key aspects of balancing solitude and social interaction include:

a) Emotional regulation: Solitude can provide opportunities for emotional processing and regulation. Research in the Journal of Adolescence found that adolescents who engaged in solitary activities for emotional regulation purposes reported better emotional well-being (Larson & Lee, 1996).

b) Creativity and problem-solving: Periods of solitude can enhance creativity and problem-solving abilities. A study in the Journal of Personality and Social Psychology demonstrated that individuals working alone generated more creative ideas than those working in groups (Goncalo & Staw, 2006).

c) Self-reflection and personal growth: Solitude provides time for introspection and self-discovery. Research in the Journal of Research in Personality found that individuals who valued solitude reported greater personal growth and self-acceptance (Long et al., 2003).

d) Social battery recharge: For introverts in particular, solitude can be crucial for recharging after social interactions. Dr. Susan Cain, author of "Quiet: The Power of Introverts in a World That Can't Stop Talking," emphasizes the importance of "restorative niches" - periods of solitude that help introverts recharge (Cain, 2012).

e) Mental health benefits of social interaction: While solitude is important, social interaction remains crucial for mental health. A study in the American Journal of Public Health found that social integration was associated with lower risk of depression (Cacioppo et al., 2006).

Strategies for balancing solitude and social interaction:

- Schedule regular alone time for self-reflection and recharging
- Practice mindfulness or meditation during solitary moments

- Engage in creative pursuits during periods of solitude
- Plan social activities that align with your energy levels and preferences
- Communicate your needs for alone time to friends and family
- Monitor your emotional state to determine when you need more solitude or social interaction

Dr. Hara Estroff Marano, Editor at Large for Psychology Today, notes: "Solitude used well can make us more capable of meaningful connection to others" (Marano, 2003).

Incorporating these social self-care rituals – nurturing relationships, setting healthy boundaries, engaging with community and support groups, and balancing solitude and social interaction – can significantly enhance emotional well-being and overall quality of life. It's important to remember that social needs can vary greatly between individuals, and finding the right balance is a personal journey that may require experimentation and self-reflection.

8

Chapter 8: Digital Detox Rituals

1. The impact of digital overload on mental health

In our increasingly connected world, digital overload has become a significant concern for mental health professionals. Excessive use of digital devices and constant connectivity can lead to various psychological and physiological issues.

Dr. Larry Rosen, Professor Emeritus of Psychology at California State University, states: "Our brains are not equipped to handle the constant barrage of information and stimuli from our digital devices. This overload can lead to anxiety, depression, and a host of other mental health issues" (Rosen, 2012).

Key aspects of digital overload's impact on mental health include:

a) Increased stress and anxiety: Constant connectivity can lead to a state of hyper vigilance. A study published in Computers in Human Behavior found that higher levels of techno-stress were associated with increased anxiety and depression symptoms (Salo et al., 2019).

b) Sleep disruption: Blue light emission from digital devices can interfere with sleep patterns. Research in the Journal of Clinical Sleep Medicine demonstrated that exposure to blue light from screens before bedtime can suppress melatonin production and disrupt circadian rhythms (Chang et al., 2015).

c) Attention deficit and cognitive overload: Frequent multitasking with digital devices can lead to cognitive overload and reduced attention span. A study in the Proceedings of the National Academy of Sciences found that heavy media multitaskers performed worse on cognitive control tasks (Ophir et al., 2009).

d) Social comparison and self-esteem issues: Social media use can contribute to negative social comparison and decreased self-esteem. Research in the Journal of Social and Clinical Psychology found a significant link between Facebook use and depressive symptoms, mediated by social comparison (Steers et al., 2014).

e) Nomophobia and addiction: Fear of being without one's mobile device (Nomophobia) and internet addiction are growing concerns. A study in Addictive Behaviors Reports found that Nomophobia was associated with increased anxiety and depression (Rodríguez-García et al., 2020).

Dr. Jean Twenge, Professor of Psychology at San Diego State University, emphasizes: "The rise in mental health issues among young adults since 2012 coincides with the widespread adoption of smartphones. While correlation doesn't prove causation, there's growing evidence that heavy digital media use is a contributing factor to the mental health crisis" (Twenge, 2017).

1. Creating healthy relationships with technology

Developing a healthy relationship with technology is crucial for maintaining mental well-being in the digital age. This involves setting boundaries, being mindful of usage, and leveraging technology to enhance rather than detract from quality of life.

Dr. Doreen Dodgen-Magee, psychologist and author of "Deviced!: Balancing Life and Technology in a Digital World," states: "A healthy tech relationship is one in which we are in control of our devices, rather than feeling controlled by them" (Dodgen-Magee, 2018).

Key aspects of creating healthy relationships with technology include:

a) Digital boundaries: Establishing clear boundaries for device use can help maintain work-life balance and reduce stress. A study in the Academy of Management Journal found that employees who set boundaries between work and personal life through email management reported lower stress and higher well-being (Barber & Santuzzi, 2015).

b) Mindful usage: Being intentional about technology use can lead to more positive outcomes. Research in the Journal of Social and Personal Relationships showed that mindful use of social media was associated with increased well-being and life satisfaction (Panger, 2018).

c) Tech-free zones and times: Designating specific areas or times as tech-free can improve face-to-face interactions and sleep quality. A study in Environment and Behavior found that the mere presence of a smartphone can negatively impact the quality of in-person conversations (Przybylski & Weinstein, 2013).

d) Positive technology use: Leveraging technology for personal growth and connection can enhance well-being. Research in Computers in Human Behavior demonstrated that using technology for self-improvement and to connect with others was associated with increased life satisfaction (Verduyn et al., 2017).

Strategies for creating healthy relationships with technology:

- Set specific times for checking emails and social media
- Use apps that track and limit screen time
- Create tech-free zones in the home, especially the bedroom
- Practice the "20-20-20" rule: Every 20 minutes, look at something

20 feet away for 20 seconds to reduce eye strain

· Engage in regular digital detox periods

Dr. Alex Soojung-Kim Pang, author of "The Distraction Addiction," emphasizes: "The goal isn't to reject technology completely, but to develop a more intentional and balanced relationship with it" (Pang, 2013).

1. **Digital detox strategies and their benefits**

Digital detox involves intentionally reducing or eliminating the use of digital devices for a period of time. This practice can provide numerous benefits for mental health, productivity, and overall well-being.

Dr. Theodora Sutton, a digital anthropologist at the University of Oxford, defines digital detox as "a period of time during which a person refrains from using electronic devices such as smartphones or computers, regarded as an opportunity to reduce stress or focus on social interaction in the physical world" (Sutton, 2017).

Key benefits of digital detox include:

a) Reduced stress and anxiety: Taking a break from constant connectivity can lower stress levels. A study in the Journal of Social Psychology found that participants who took a break from Facebook for just five days reported lower cortisol levels (Vanman et al., 2018).

b) Improved sleep quality: Reducing screen time, especially before bed, can enhance sleep quality. Research in Sleep Health demonstrated that a digital detox before bedtime improved both sleep duration and quality (Perrault et al., 2019).

c) Enhanced face-to-face interactions: Digital detoxes can improve the quality of in-person relationships. A study in Cyberpsychology, Behavior, and Social Networking found that abstaining from social media led to increased life satisfaction and more in-person social interaction (Hunt et al., 2018).

d) Increased productivity and focus: Taking breaks from digital devices can improve concentration and productivity. Research in the Journal of Experimental Psychology: Human Perception and Performance showed that even brief digital detoxes can improve cognitive performance (Atchley & Strayer, 2017).

e) Greater self-awareness: Digital detoxes provide opportunities for self-reflection and mindfulness. A study in the Journal of Travel Research found that digital-free tourism experiences led to increased self-awareness and mindfulness (Li et al., 2018).

Effective digital detox strategies:

- Start with short periods of digital abstinence and gradually increase duration
- Engage in outdoor activities or nature retreats without devices
- Practice device-free meals or social gatherings
- Designate specific days (e.g., "Tech-Free Tuesdays") for regular digital detoxes
- Use apps or settings to limit device usage during certain hours

Dr. Cal Newport, author of "Digital Minimalism," advocates for a 30-day digital declutter: "The key is to step away from optional technologies for 30 days so you can reset your digital life. When the period ends, you reintroduce technology intentionally and on your own terms" (Newport, 2019).

1. **Mindful use of social media**

Mindful use of social media involves being intentional and aware of how, when, and why we engage with these platforms. This approach can help mitigate the negative effects of social media while maximizing its potential benefits.

Dr. Erin Vogel, postdoctoral fellow in the Department of Psychiatry at the University of California, San Francisco, states: "Mindful use of social media means being aware of your motivations for using it, how it affects your emotions, and whether it's adding value to your life" (Vogel et al., 2020).

Key aspects of mindful social media use include:

a) Awareness of emotional responses: Being cognizant of how social media affects your mood is crucial. A study in the Journal of Social and Clinical Psychology found that limiting social media use to 30 minutes per day led to significant reductions in loneliness and depression (Hunt et al., 2018).

b) Intentional engagement: Using social media with purpose rather than out of habit or boredom can lead to more positive outcomes. Research in Information, Communication & Society showed that using Facebook for direct communication was associated with improvements in well-being, while passive use was not (Burke & Kraut, 2016).

c) Curating a positive feed: Actively shaping your social media environment can improve your online experience. A study in New Media & Society found that exposure to positive content on social media was associated with increased positive affect (Kramer et al., 2014).

d) Balancing online and offline interactions: Ensuring that social media complements rather than replaces in-person interactions is important. Research in the Journal of Computer-Mediated Communication demonstrated that social media use that facilitates offline social interactions was associated with increased well-being (Shen et al., 2017).

Strategies for mindful social media use:

- Set specific times for checking social media and stick to them
- Turn off push notifications to reduce the urge for constant checking
- Regularly audit your friend/follow lists and unfollow accounts that

don't add value
- Practice the "scroll, stop, and reflect" technique: Pause while scrolling to consider how the content makes you feel
- Use features like Instagram's "You're All Caught Up" to set natural stopping points

Dr. Brian Primack, Dean of the College of Education and Health Professions at the University of Arkansas, emphasizes: "It's not about completely avoiding social media, but rather using it in a way that enhances rather than detracts from your life" (Primack et al., 2017).

Incorporating these digital detox rituals – understanding the impact of digital overload, creating healthy relationships with technology, implementing digital detox strategies, and practicing mindful use of social media – can significantly improve mental well-being in our increasingly digital world. It's important to remember that finding the right balance is a personal journey that may require experimentation and regular reassessment.

9

Chapter 9: Nature and Environmental Self-Care

1. **The psychological benefits of nature exposure**

Exposure to nature has been consistently shown to have significant positive effects on mental health and overall well-being. This connection, often referred to as "biophilia," suggests that humans have an innate affinity for nature and other living things.

Dr. Ming Kuo, Director of the Landscape and Human Health Laboratory at the University of Illinois, states: "The strength of the evidence for nature's benefits to health and well-being is actually quite shocking. It's on par with other things that we know are good for us, like eating fruits and vegetables and getting a good night's sleep" (Kuo, 2015).

Key psychological benefits of nature exposure include:

a) Stress reduction: Exposure to natural environments has been shown to lower stress levels. A study published in the International Journal of Environmental Research and Public Health found that as little as 10 minutes in a natural setting can significantly reduce stress (Hunter et al., 2019).

b) Improved mood: Nature exposure is associated with increased positive emotions and decreased negative emotions. Research in the Journal of Positive Psychology demonstrated that participants who spent time in nature reported higher levels of happiness and lower levels of negative affect (Capaldi et al., 2014).

c) Enhanced cognitive function: Time in nature can improve attention and cognitive performance. A study in Psychological Science found that walking in nature improved performance on tasks requiring directed-attention abilities (Berman et al., 2008).

d) Increased creativity: Nature exposure has been linked to enhanced creative thinking. Research in PLOS ONE showed that participants who spent four days immersed in nature scored 50% higher on a creative problem-solving task (Atchley et al., 2012).

e) Reduced symptoms of anxiety and depression: Regular nature exposure can alleviate symptoms of mental health disorders. A meta-analysis published in the Journal of Affective Disorders found that nature-based interventions were effective in reducing symptoms of anxiety and depression (Koselka et al., 2021).

Dr. Mathew White, environmental psychologist at the University of Exeter, emphasizes: "We find that people who spend at least two hours a week in nature are significantly more likely to report good health and higher psychological wellbeing than those who don't visit nature at all" (White et al., 2019).

Strategies for increasing nature exposure:

- Take regular walks in local parks or green spaces
- Practice "forest bathing" or mindful nature walks
- Incorporate nature into daily commutes when possible
- Plan outdoor activities or vacations in natural settings
- Use lunch breaks to spend time outdoors

1. Creating a nurturing home environment

The physical environment in which we live can significantly impact our mental health and overall well-being. Creating a nurturing home environment involves designing spaces that promote relaxation, productivity, and positive emotions.

Dr. Sally Augustin, an environmental psychologist, states: "Our physical surroundings have a significant impact on our cognition, emotions, and behavior, often without our being aware of them" (Augustin, 2009).

Key aspects of creating a nurturing home environment include:

a) Natural light: Exposure to natural light is crucial for maintaining healthy circadian rhythms and mood. A study in the Journal of Clinical Sleep Medicine found that workers with more natural light exposure in the office had better sleep quality and overall health outcomes (Boubekri et al., 2014).

b) Color psychology: The colors in our environment can affect our mood and behavior. Research in the journal Color Research and Application showed that blue and green hues were associated with feelings of calmness and relaxation (Elliot, 2015).

c) Decluttering: A tidy, organized space can reduce stress and improve focus. A study in Current Psychology found that clutter was associated with decreased life satisfaction and increased stress (Roster et al., 2016).

d) Personalization: Incorporating meaningful personal items can create a sense of comfort and identity. Research in the Journal of Environmental Psychology demonstrated that personalization of workspace was associated with increased job satisfaction and well-being (Wells, 2000).

e) Ergonomics: Proper ergonomics can prevent physical discomfort and associated stress. A study in the International Journal of Industrial Ergonomics found that ergonomic interventions in the home office improved both physical and mental well-being (Karakolis & Callaghan, 2014).

Strategies for creating a nurturing home environment:

- Maximize natural light through window treatments and strategic furniture placement
- Use calming colors in bedrooms and relaxation areas
- Implement regular decluttering routines
- Create dedicated spaces for different activities (work, relaxation, hobbies)
- Invest in ergonomic furniture and proper lighting for work areas

Dr. Toby Israel, design psychologist and author of "Some Place Like Home," emphasizes: "Our homes should be more than just functional spaces. They should be environments that nurture our psychological well-being and help us become our best selves" (Israel, 2003).

1. Indoor plants and their impact on mental health

Incorporating indoor plants into living and working spaces has been shown to have numerous benefits for mental health and cognitive function. This practice, often referred to as "indoor biophilia," can significantly improve the quality of indoor environments.

Dr. Tove Fjeld, a professor at the Norwegian University of Life Sciences, states: "Indoor plants can reduce stress levels, increase productivity, and improve well-being in ways that are valuable for a healthy indoor climate" (Fjeld, 2000).

Key benefits of indoor plants for mental health include:

a) Stress reduction: The presence of indoor plants has been associated with lower stress levels. A study in the Journal of Physiological Anthropology found that interacting with indoor plants can reduce physiological and psychological stress (Lee et al., 2015).

b) Improved air quality: Many indoor plants can help purify air by removing toxins. The classic NASA Clean Air Study demonstrated that certain indoor plants could remove significant amounts of indoor air pollutants (Wolverton et al., 1989).

c) Enhanced cognitive function: The presence of plants in work environments has been linked to improved cognitive performance. Research in the Journal of Environmental Psychology found that the presence of plants in an office setting increased productivity and attention capacity (Raanaas et al., 2011).

d) Mood elevation: Caring for plants can provide a sense of accomplishment and improve mood. A study in Urban Forestry & Urban Greening showed that interacting with indoor plants can reduce psychological and physiological stress (Toyoda et al., 2020).

e) Increased creativity: Plants in the workspace have been associated with enhanced creativity. A study in the Journal of Environmental Psychology found that the presence of plants in an office environment was associated with increased creative performance (Shibata & Suzuki, 2004).

Recommended indoor plants for mental health benefits:

- Snake Plant (Sansevieria trifasciata)
- Peace Lily (Spathiphyllum)
- Spider Plant (Chlorophytum comosum)
- Aloe Vera
- English Ivy (Hedera helix)

Dr. Virginia Lohr, Professor of Horticulture at Washington State University, emphasizes: "Interior plants can provide a way for people to experience nature and receive some of its benefits in settings where this might not otherwise be possible" (Lohr, 2010).

1. **Eco-friendly practices for mental wellbeing**

Engaging in Eco-friendly practices can have significant positive impacts on mental health and well-being. These practices not only benefit the environment but also provide a sense of purpose, connection, and personal satisfaction.

Dr. Susan Clayton, Professor of Psychology at the College of Wooster, states: "Engaging in environmentally friendly behaviors can increase our sense of competence and control, which are important for mental health" (Clayton, 2012).

Key aspects of Eco-friendly practices and their mental health benefits include:

a) Sense of purpose: Environmental activism and eco-friendly behaviors can provide a sense of meaning and purpose. Research in the Journal of Environmental Psychology found that pro-environmental behavior was associated with increased life satisfaction and positive affect (Venhoeven et al., 2013).

b) Connection to nature: Eco-friendly practices often involve increased interaction with nature, which has numerous mental health benefits. A study in Environment and Behavior demonstrated that connection to nature was associated with increased psychological well-being (Nisbet et al., 2011).

c) Reduced Eco-anxiety: Taking action to address environmental concerns can help alleviate Eco-anxiety. Research in Global Environmental Change found that engagement in pro-environmental behaviors was associated with reduced climate anxiety (Helm et al., 2018).

d) Community engagement: Many Eco-friendly practices involve community participation, which can enhance social connections. A study in the Journal of Environmental Psychology showed that community-based environmental initiatives were associated with increased social cohesion and well-being (Dinnie et al., 2013).

e) Physical activity: Many Eco-friendly practices, such as gardening or cycling, involve physical activity, which has well-established mental health benefits. Research in Preventive Medicine found that active transportation was associated with improved mental health (Martin et al., 2014).

Eco-friendly practices that can promote mental wellbeing:

- Gardening and growing own food
- Participating in community clean-up events
- Adopting a minimalist lifestyle
- Practicing mindful consumption
- Using active transportation (walking, cycling)
- Engaging in upcycling or DIY projects

Dr. Sabine Pahl, Professor of Urban and Environmental Psychology at the University of Vienna, emphasizes: "Sustainable behaviors can create a positive feedback loop: they make us feel good, which in turn motivates us to engage in more sustainable behaviors" (Pahl et al., 2017).

Incorporating these nature and environmental self-care practices – regular nature exposure, creating a nurturing home environment, incorporating indoor plants, and engaging in Eco-friendly practices – can significantly enhance mental well-being. These practices not only benefit individual health but also contribute to the health of our planet, creating a positive cycle of personal and environmental well-being.

10

Chapter 10: Spiritual Self-Care Rituals

1. Defining spirituality in the context of self-care

Spirituality in the context of self-care encompasses a broad range of practices and beliefs that contribute to a sense of meaning, purpose, and connection beyond the self. It's important to note that spirituality doesn't necessarily equate to religiosity, although for many, religious practices are a significant part of their spiritual self-care.

Dr. Christina Puchalski, Director of the George Washington Institute for Spirituality and Health, defines spirituality as "the aspect of humanity that refers to the way individuals seek and express meaning and purpose and the way they experience their connectedness to the moment, to self, to others, to nature, and to the significant or sacred" (Puchalski et al., 2009).

Key aspects of spirituality in self-care include:

a) Meaning-making: Spirituality often involves the process of finding meaning in life experiences. Research in the Journal of Religion and Health found that spiritual meaning-making was associated with better mental health outcomes, particularly in coping with adversity (Park,

66

2013).

b) Transcendence: Spiritual practices often involve experiences that transcend everyday consciousness. A study in Psychology of Religion and Spirituality demonstrated that transcendent experiences were associated with increased well-being and life satisfaction (Van Cappellen & Saroglou, 2012).

c) Connectedness: Spirituality often fosters a sense of connection to others, nature, or a higher power. Research in the Journal of Happiness Studies found that spiritual connectedness was a significant predictor of subjective well-being (Ivtzan et al., 2013).

d) Personal growth: Spiritual practices often encourage self-reflection and personal development. A study in the Journal of Positive Psychology showed that spiritual growth was associated with increased psychological well-being (Wink & Dillon, 2003).

Dr. Lisa Miller, Professor of Psychology and Education at Columbia University, emphasizes: "Spirituality is a powerful aspect of human experience that can greatly enhance our capacity for joy, resilience, and compassion" (Miller, 2015).

When incorporating spirituality into self-care practices, it's important to:

- Recognize that spirituality is deeply personal and can take many forms
- Explore various spiritual practices to find what resonates
- Respect diverse spiritual beliefs and practices
- Understand that spiritual self-care can evolve over time

1. **Meditation and contemplative practices**

Meditation and contemplative practices are cornerstone techniques in spiritual self-care, offering numerous benefits for mental, emotional, and physical well-being.

Dr. Jon Kabat-Zinn, founder of Mindfulness-Based Stress Reduction (MBSR), defines mindfulness meditation as "paying attention in a particular way: on purpose, in the present moment, and non-judgmentally" (Kabat-Zinn, 1994).

Key benefits of meditation and contemplative practices include:

a) Stress reduction: Regular meditation practice has been shown to reduce stress levels. A meta-analysis published in the Journal of Psychosomatic Research found that mindfulness meditation programs had moderate evidence of improving anxiety and depression (Goyal et al., 2014).

b) Improved emotional regulation: Meditation can enhance our ability to manage emotions. Research in Frontiers in Human Neuroscience demonstrated that mindfulness meditation training altered brain regions involved in emotional regulation (Tang et al., 2015).

c) Enhanced cognitive function: Regular meditation practice has been associated with improved attention and cognitive flexibility. A study in Psychological Science found that intensive meditation training improved performance on tasks of sustained attention (MacLean et al., 2010).

d) Increased self-awareness: Contemplative practices often lead to greater self-understanding. Research in the Journal of Positive Psychology showed that mindfulness meditation increased self-insight and reduced psychological distress (Xu et al., 2017).

e) Physical health benefits: Meditation has been linked to various physical health improvements. A study in Psych neuroendocrinology found that mindfulness meditation was associated with reduced inflammation markers (Creswell et al., 2016).

Types of meditation and contemplative practices:

- Mindfulness meditation

- Loving-kindness meditation
- Transcendental Meditation
- Centering prayer
- Contemplative reading (Lectio Divina)
- Body scan meditation
- Walking meditation

Dr. Richard Davidson, founder of the Center for Healthy Minds at the University of Wisconsin-Madison, states: "We can actually train our minds to change our brains in ways that may promote well-being" (Davidson & Begley, 2012).

1. **Exploring personal values and purpose**

Exploring and aligning with one's personal values and sense of purpose is a crucial aspect of spiritual self-care. This process involves introspection, self-reflection, and often, a reevaluation of life priorities.

Dr. Viktor Frankl, neurologist, psychiatrist, and Holocaust survivor, emphasized the importance of finding meaning in life: "Man's search for meaning is the primary motivation in his life and not a 'secondary rationalization' of instinctual drives" (Frankl, 1946).

Key aspects of exploring personal values and purpose include:

a) Self-reflection: Regularly examining one's beliefs, motivations, and actions can lead to greater self-understanding. A study in the Journal of Personality and Social Psychology found that self-reflection was associated with greater purpose in life and self-concept clarity (Trapnell & Campbell, 1999).

b) Value clarification: Identifying and prioritizing personal values can guide decision-making and behavior. Research in the Journal of Personality showed that value clarity was associated with greater well-being and life satisfaction (Schwartz & Sortheix, 2018).

c) Goal setting: Aligning goals with personal values and purpose can increase motivation and life satisfaction. A study in the Journal of Happiness Studies found that pursuing self-concordant goals (those aligned with personal values) was associated with greater well-being (Sheldon & Elliot, 1999).

d) Meaning-making: Finding meaning in daily experiences and challenges can enhance resilience and well-being. Research in the Journal of Positive Psychology demonstrated that meaning-making coping strategies were associated with post-traumatic growth (Park, 2010).

Strategies for exploring personal values and purpose:

- Journaling exercises focused on life experiences and lessons learned
- Creating a personal mission statement
- Engaging in value sort exercises
- Participating in purpose workshops or retreats
- Regular reflection on how daily activities align with personal values

Dr. Emily Esfahani Smith, author of "The Power of Meaning," emphasizes: "The search for meaning is not about finding a clear-cut answer to the question, 'What is the meaning of life?' It's about figuring out what matters to you" (Smith, 2017).

1. **Rituals for connecting with something greater than oneself**

Rituals that foster a connection with something greater than oneself are integral to many spiritual traditions and can be powerful tools for spiritual self-care. These practices can provide a sense of awe, transcendence, and interconnectedness.

Dr. Dacher Keltner, professor of psychology at UC Berkeley, states: "Experiences of awe, wonder, and joy connect us to the greater tapestry of life and enhance our sense of well-being" (Keltner, 2016).

Key aspects of rituals for connecting with something greater include:

a) Awe experiences: Engaging in activities that inspire awe can promote well-being. Research in the Journal of Personality and Social Psychology found that awe experiences were associated with increased life satisfaction and prosocial behavior (Rudd et al., 2012).

b) Nature connection: Spending time in nature can foster a sense of connection to something greater. A study in the Journal of Environmental Psychology showed that nature experiences were associated with increased feelings of connectedness and well-being (Mayer et al., 2009).

c) Collective rituals: Participating in group rituals can foster a sense of community and transcendence. Research in Psychological Science demonstrated that synchronous activities (like group singing or dancing) increased pain tolerance and feelings of social connection (Tarr et al., 2015).

d) Contemplation of existence: Reflecting on one's place in the universe can provide perspective and meaning. A study in the Journal of Positive Psychology found that cosmic outlook (considering one's place in the universe) was associated with increased meaning in life (Lebedev et al., 2020).

Rituals for connecting with something greater:

- Stargazing and contemplating the cosmos
- Participating in religious or spiritual ceremonies
- Engaging in group meditation or prayer
- Creating or appreciating art
- Volunteering or engaging spin acts of service
- Practicing gratitude for life's interconnectedness

Dr. Barbara Fredrickson, Professor of Psychology at the University of North Carolina at Chapel Hill, emphasizes: "Love and other positive emotions open our hearts and our minds, making us more receptive and more creative" (Fredrickson, 2013).

Incorporating these spiritual self-care rituals – defining personal spirituality, practicing meditation and contemplation, exploring values and purpose, and engaging in rituals that connect with something greater – can significantly enhance overall well-being. These practices offer ways to find meaning, cultivate inner peace, and foster a sense of connectedness in our lives. It's important to approach spiritual self-care with an open mind, respecting diverse beliefs and finding practices that resonate personally.

Chapter 11: Creative Self-Care Rituals

1. **The mental health benefits of creative expression**

Creative expression has been recognized as a powerful tool for maintaining and improving mental health. Engaging in creative activities can provide a range of psychological benefits, from stress reduction to improved emotional regulation.

Dr. Christianne Strang, a board-certified art therapist and past president of the American Art Therapy Association, states: "Creativity in and of itself is important for remaining healthy, remaining connected to yourself and connected to the world" (Strang, 2018).

Key mental health benefits of creative expression include:

a) Stress reduction: Creative activities can significantly lower stress levels. A study published in Art Therapy found that 45 minutes of creative activity significantly reduced cortisol levels, regardless of artistic experience or talent (Kaimal et al., 2016).

b) Improved mood: Engaging in creative pursuits can boost positive emotions. Research in the Journal of Positive Psychology demonstrated that engaging in small creative projects daily led to increased positive affect and flourishing (Conner et al., 2018).

c) Enhanced cognitive function: Creative activities can improve cognitive flexibility and problem-solving skills. A study in Creativity Research Journal found that engaging in creative writing enhanced cognitive function in older adults (Palmiero et al., 2016).

d) Increased self-awareness: Creative expression can facilitate self-discovery and introspection. Research in Psychology of Aesthetics, Creativity, and the Arts showed that expressive writing increased self-awareness and personal growth (Lowe, 2006).

e) Improved emotional regulation: Creative activities can help process and regulate emotions. A study in the British Journal of Clinical Psychology found that art-making helped improve mood regulation in individuals with mental health issues (Thayer & Lane, 2000).

Dr. James C. Kaufman, professor of educational psychology at the University of Connecticut, emphasizes: "Engaging in creative activities is not just a fun way to pass time; it's a vital component of psychological well-being" (Kaufman, 2018).

1. **Incorporating daily creative practices**

Integrating creative practices into daily routines can provide consistent access to the mental health benefits of creativity. These practices don't need to be time-consuming or elaborate to be effective.

Dr. Ruth Richards, a professor of psychology at Saybrook University, states: "Everyday creativity can be as simple as trying a new recipe or rearranging your living room. It's about approaching life with flexibility and openness" (Richards, 2007).

Strategies for incorporating daily creative practices:

a) Morning pages: Developed by Julia Cameron, this practice involves writing three pages of stream-of-consciousness thoughts each morning. Research in the Journal of Poetry Therapy found that expressive writing practices like morning pages can improve emotional well-being (Pennebaker, 1997).

b) Micro-creativity: Engage in small creative acts throughout the day, such as doodling during phone calls or arranging your lunch attractively. A study in the Journal of Occupational and Organizational Psychology found that small creative activities during the workday can boost problem-solving skills and work engagement (Eschleman et al., 2014).

c) Creative rituals: Establish a regular time for creative activities, such as sketching for 15 minutes before bed. Research in Thinking Skills and Creativity showed that establishing creative routines can enhance overall creative output (Botella et al., 2018).

d) Mindful observation: Practice seeing the world creatively by noticing details, colors, and patterns in your environment. A study in Psychology of Aesthetics, Creativity, and the Arts found that mindfulness practices can enhance creative thinking (Lebuda et al., 2016).

e) Creative journaling: Combine writing and visual elements in a journal. Research in the Journal of Poetry Therapy demonstrated that creative journaling can improve emotional expression and self-understanding (Adams, 1999).

Dr. Shelley Carson, lecturer in psychology at Harvard University, emphasizes: "Creativity is not a 'use it or lose it' phenomenon. The more you practice creative thinking, the better you become at it" (Carson, 2010).

1. Overcoming creative blocks

Creative blocks can be frustrating and may hinder the mental health benefits of creative practices. Understanding and addressing these blocks is crucial for maintaining a consistent creative practice.

Dr. Scott Barry Kaufman, scientific director of the Imagination

Institute at the University of Pennsylvania, states: "Creative blocks often stem from fear, perfectionism, or a fixed mindset about creativity" (Kaufman, 2013).

Strategies for overcoming creative blocks:

a) Embrace imperfection: Allow yourself to create without judgment. Research in Thinking Skills and Creativity found that a willingness to make mistakes and learn from them is associated with higher creative achievement (Beghetto, 2014).

b) Change your environment: Work in a new location or rearrange your creative space. A study in the Journal of Environmental Psychology demonstrated that changes in physical environment can stimulate creative thinking (McCoy & Evans, 2002).

c) Practice divergent thinking: Engage in exercises that encourage multiple solutions to a problem. Research in Psychology of Aesthetics, Creativity, and the Arts showed that regular practice of divergent thinking can enhance overall creativity (Sun et al., 2016).

d) Set realistic goals: Break large projects into smaller, manageable tasks. A study in Organizational Behavior and Human Decision Processes found that setting specific, challenging but achievable goals can enhance creative performance (Shalley, 1995).

e) Use constraints: Paradoxically, working within constraints can boost creativity. Research in the Journal of Consumer Research found that resource constraints can lead to more creative outputs (Moreau & Dahl, 2005).

Dr. Teresa Amabile, professor at Harvard Business School, emphasizes: "Progress in meaningful work is the single most important factor in boosting emotions, motivation, and perceptions during a workday" (Amabile & Kramer, 2011).

1. **Using art, music, or writing as therapy**

Art, music, and writing can be powerful therapeutic tools, offering unique ways to process emotions, trauma, and experiences. These creative therapies are increasingly recognized in clinical settings for their effectiveness in promoting mental health.

Dr. Cathy Malchiodi, art therapist and author, states: "Creative therapies provide a way to communicate and heal that goes beyond words, tapping into emotions and experiences that may be difficult to express verbally" (Malchiodi, 2020).

Key aspects of creative therapies:

a) Art therapy: Uses the creative process of art-making to improve mental health. A meta-analysis in The Arts in Psychotherapy found that art therapy was effective in reducing depression symptoms across various populations (Blomdahl et al., 2013).

b) Music therapy: Utilizes music to address physical, emotional, and social needs. Research in the Journal of Music Therapy demonstrated that music therapy can reduce anxiety and improve mood in patients with depression (Erkkilä et al., 2011).

c) Writing therapy: Involves expressive writing to process experiences and emotions. A study in the Journal of Clinical Psychology found that expressive writing interventions were effective in reducing symptoms of post-traumatic stress disorder (PTSD) (Sloan et al., 2011).

d) Drama therapy: Uses theatrical techniques to facilitate personal growth and healing. Research in The Arts in Psychotherapy showed that drama therapy can improve social skills and reduce anxiety in children with autism spectrum disorders (D'Amico et al., 2015).

e) Dance/movement therapy: Utilizes movement to promote emotional, social, cognitive, and physical integration. A study in Frontiers in Psychology found that dance/movement therapy was effective in treating depression and anxiety (Koch et al., 2019).

Dr. Girija Kaimal, associate professor in the Creative Arts Therapies Department at Drexel University, emphasizes: "Art therapy isn't about becoming a great artist, it's about expressing yourself authentically and using creativity as a pathway to well-being" (Kaimal, 2019).

Incorporating these creative self-care rituals – recognizing the mental health benefits of creativity, establishing daily creative practices, overcoming creative blocks, and engaging in creative therapies – can significantly enhance overall well-being. These practices offer powerful tools for self-expression, emotional processing, and personal growth. Remember that creativity is a skill that can be developed, and the focus should be on the process rather than the product. By nurturing our creative selves, we open up new pathways for healing, growth, and self-discovery.

12

Chapter 12: Professional Self-Care Rituals

1. Managing work-related stress

Work-related stress is a significant concern in modern professional life, with potential impacts on both mental and physical health. Effective stress management is crucial for maintaining well-being and productivity in the workplace.

Dr. Christina Maslach, Professor Emerita of Psychology at the University of California, Berkeley, states: "Job burnout is a prolonged response to chronic emotional and interpersonal stressors on the job" (Maslach et al., 2001).

Key strategies for managing work-related stress include:

a) Time management: Effective time management can reduce feelings of being overwhelmed. A study in the Journal of Occupational Health Psychology found that time management training significantly reduced work-related stress and increased job satisfaction (Häfner & Stock, 2010).

b) Mindfulness practices: Incorporating mindfulness into the workday can help manage stress. Research in the Journal of Occupational Health Psychology demonstrated that a workplace mindfulness-based intervention reduced perceived stress and improved sleep quality (Wolever et al., 2012).

c) Regular breaks: Taking short, frequent breaks can help maintain focus and reduce stress. A study in Cognition found that brief diversions from a task can dramatically improve one's ability to focus on that task for prolonged periods (Ariga & Lleras, 2011).

d) Physical activity: Incorporating exercise into the workday can reduce stress. Research in the International Journal of Workplace Health Management showed that even short bouts of workplace physical activity can improve mood and perceived work performance (Coulson et al., 2008).

e) Cognitive reframing: Changing how one perceives stressful situations can alter the stress response. A study in the Journal of Personality and Social Psychology found that reframing stress as enhancing rather than debilitating led to improved performance under pressure (Crum et al., 2013).

Dr. Robert Sapolsky, Professor of Biology and Neurology at Stanford University, emphasizes: "Stress is not inherently bad. It's chronic, uncontrollable stress that is damaging. Learning to manage and channel stress effectively is key to professional well-being" (Sapolsky, 2004).

1. **Creating a supportive work environment**

A supportive work environment is crucial for professional well-being and can significantly impact job satisfaction, productivity, and overall mental health.

Dr. Amy Edmondson, Professor of Leadership and Management at Harvard Business School, states: "Psychological safety – the belief that one can speak up without risk of punishment or humiliation – is a key characteristic of high-performing teams" (Edmondson, 1999).

Key aspects of creating a supportive work environment include:

a) Open communication: Fostering an environment where employees feel comfortable expressing ideas and concerns. Research in the Journal of Applied Psychology found that open communication was positively associated with job satisfaction and organizational commitment (Ng & Feldman, 2012).

b) Work-life balance: Promoting policies that support work-life balance. A study in the International Journal of Human Resource Management showed that work-life balance initiatives were associated with increased job satisfaction and reduced turnover intentions (Beauregard & Henry, 2009).

c) Recognition and appreciation: Regularly acknowledging employee contributions. Research in the Journal of Organizational Behavior demonstrated that perceived organizational support, including recognition, was positively related to job performance and negatively related to withdrawal behaviors (Rhoades & Eisenberger, 2002).

d) Professional autonomy: Providing employees with a sense of control over their work. A meta-analysis in the Journal of Applied Psychology found that job autonomy was positively related to job satisfaction, performance, and motivation (Humphrey et al., 2007).

e) Social support: Encouraging positive relationships among colleagues. A study in Work & Stress showed that coworker support was associated with reduced job stress and increased job satisfaction (Chiaburu & Harrison, 2008).

Dr. Adam Grant, Professor of Management at the Wharton School, University of Pennsylvania, emphasizes: "The most meaningful way to succeed is to help others succeed" (Grant, 2013).

1. **Professional development as self-care**

Engaging in professional development can be a form of self-care, contributing to personal growth, job satisfaction, and career advancement.

Dr. Carol Dweck, Professor of Psychology at Stanford University, states: "In a growth mindset, challenges are exciting rather than threatening. So rather than thinking, oh, I'm going to reveal my weaknesses, you say, wow, here's a chance to grow" (Dweck, 2006).

Key aspects of professional development as self-care include:

a) Continuous learning: Engaging in ongoing education and skill development. A study in the Journal of Vocational Behavior found that continuous learning was positively associated with career satisfaction and employability (De Vos et al., 2011).

b) Goal setting: Setting and working towards professional goals. Research in the Academy of Management Journal demonstrated that setting specific, challenging goals led to higher performance than vague or easy goals (Locke & Latham, 2002).

c) Mentorship: Seeking or providing mentorship. A meta-analysis in the Journal of Applied Psychology found that mentoring was associated with a range of favorable behavioral, attitudinal, health-related, relational, motivational, and career outcomes (Eby et al., 2008).

d) Networking: Building professional relationships. A study in the Journal of Applied Psychology showed that networking behaviors were positively related to career success (Wolff & Moser, 2009).

e) Reflection and self-assessment: Regularly reflecting on professional growth and areas for improvement. Research in Personnel Psychology found that self-awareness was positively related to managerial effectiveness and career success (Church, 1997).

Dr. Peter Senge, senior lecturer at MIT Sloan School of Management, emphasizes: "The only sustainable competitive advantage is an organization's ability to learn faster than the competition" (Senge, 1990).

1. **Balancing ambition and well-being**

While ambition can drive professional success, it's crucial to balance it with personal well-being to avoid burnout and maintain long-term career satisfaction.

Dr. Manfred F.R. Kets de Vries, Distinguished Clinical Professor of Leadership Development and Organizational Change at INSEAD, states: "While ambition can be the engine of achievement, unchecked ambition can lead to a host of problems, including burnout, damaged relationships, and ethical lapses" (Kets de Vries, 2014).

Key strategies for balancing ambition and well-being include:

a) Setting realistic goals: Ensuring that professional goals are challenging yet achievable. A study in the Journal of Applied Psychology found that setting overly ambitious goals can lead to unethical behavior and burnout (Welsh & Ordóñez, 2014).

b) Practicing self-compassion: Being kind to oneself, especially in the face of failure or setbacks. Research in the Journal of Personality and Social Psychology demonstrated that self-compassion was associated with greater personal initiative, perceived competence, and motivation to learn and grow (Neff et al., 2005).

c) Maintaining work-life boundaries: Establishing clear boundaries between work and personal life. A study in the Journal of Occupational Health Psychology found that psychological detachment from work during non-work time was crucial for employee well-being and work engagement (Sonnentag et al., 2010).

d) Cultivating non-work interests: Engaging in hobbies and activities outside of work. Research in the Journal of Occupational and Organizational Psychology showed that leisure activities contributed to recovery from job stress and improved well-being (Sonnentag, 2012).

e) Regular self-reflection: Periodically reassessing career goals and their alignment with personal values. A study in the Academy of Management Learning & Education found that reflective practice was associated with improved leadership skills and career satisfaction

(DeRue et al., 2012).

Dr. Brené Brown, research professor at the University of Houston, emphasizes: "Healthy striving is self-focused: How can I improve? Perfectionism is other-focused: What will they think?" (Brown, 2010).

Incorporating these professional self-care rituals – managing work-related stress, creating a supportive work environment, engaging in professional development, and balancing ambition with well-being – can significantly enhance career satisfaction and overall life quality. These practices offer powerful tools for navigating the challenges of professional life while maintaining personal health and happiness. Remember that professional self-care is not a luxury but a necessity for sustainable career success and personal fulfillment. By prioritizing these practices, professionals can cultivate resilience, foster growth, and achieve a harmonious integration of work and life.

13

Chapter 13: Customizing Your Self-Care Revolution

1. Creating a personalized self-care plan

Developing a personalized self-care plan is crucial for ensuring that self-care practices are effective, sustainable, and aligned with individual needs and preferences.

Dr. Kristin Neff, Associate Professor of Educational Psychology at the University of Texas at Austin, states: "Self-care isn't one-size-fits-all. It's about knowing what you need to feel cared for and deliberately putting those things into practice" (Neff, 2011).

Key steps in creating a personalized self-care plan include:

a) Self-assessment: Evaluate current stressors, coping mechanisms, and areas for improvement. A study in the Journal of Counseling Psychology found that self-awareness was a key factor in developing effective self-care strategies (Myers et al., 2012).

b) Identifying personal values: Align self-care practices with core values for greater motivation and sustainability. Research in the Journal of Personality and Social Psychology demonstrated that value-aligned activities led to greater well-being and life satisfaction (Sheldon & Elliot, 1999).

c) Setting SMART goals: Develop Specific, Measurable, Achievable, Relevant, and Time-bound self-care goals. A meta-analysis in Psychological Bulletin showed that setting specific and challenging goals led to higher performance than vague or easy goals (Locke & Latham, 2002).

d) Diversifying practices: Include a mix of physical, emotional, social, and spiritual self-care activities. A study in the Journal of Positive Psychology found that a multi-dimensional approach to well-being was more effective than focusing on a single area (Huppert & So, 2013).

e) Scheduling and integration: Incorporate self-care activities into daily routines. Research in the British Journal of Health Psychology showed that habits formed more quickly when tied to existing routines (Lally et al., 2010).

Dr. Alex Korb, neuroscientist and author, emphasizes: "The key is to start small. Pick one or two practices that resonate with you and make them a consistent part of your routine before adding more" (Korb, 2015).

1. **Overcoming obstacles to consistent self-care**

Identifying and addressing barriers to consistent self-care is essential for maintaining a sustainable self-care practice.

Dr. Kelly McGonigal, health psychologist and lecturer at Stanford University, states: "The biggest obstacles to self-care are often psychological – guilt, perfectionism, and the belief that self-care is selfish" (McGonigal, 2013).

Common obstacles and strategies to overcome them include:

a) Time constraints: Prioritize and schedule self-care activities. A study in the Journal of Occupational Health Psychology found that time management training significantly improved work-life balance and reduced stress (Häfner & Stock, 2010).

b) Guilt: Reframe self-care as essential for overall well-being and ability to care for others. Research in Personality and Social Psychology Bulletin showed that self-compassion was associated with greater personal improvement motivation (Breines & Chen, 2012).

c) Lack of motivation: Start with small, achievable goals to build momentum. A study in the European Journal of Social Psychology found that it takes an average of 66 days to form a new habit (Lally et al., 2010).

d) Perfectionism: Focus on progress rather than perfection. Research in Cognitive Therapy and Research demonstrated that perfectionistic attitudes were associated with increased stress and burnout (D'Souza et al., 2011).

e) Environmental barriers: Create a supportive environment for self-care. A study in the Annual Review of Psychology showed that environmental cues significantly influence behavior change (Wood & Neal, 2007).

Dr. Kristin Neff emphasizes: "Remember that self-care isn't selfish. It's like putting on your own oxygen mask first – you can't effectively help others if you're not taking care of yourself" (Neff, 2011).

1. **Adapting self-care practices for different life stages**

Self-care needs evolve throughout different life stages, requiring adaptations to maintain effectiveness and relevance.

Dr. Vivek Murthy, 19th Surgeon General of the United States, states: "Our self-care practices should evolve as we do, reflecting the changing demands and priorities of each life stage" (Murthy, 2020).

Key considerations for adapting self-care practices include:

a) Young adulthood: Focus on establishing healthy habits and coping mechanisms. Research in the Journal of Youth and Adolescence found that developing self-care skills in young adulthood was associated with better mental health outcomes later in life (Conley et al., 2013).

b) Parenthood: Emphasize efficient, flexible self-care strategies. A study in the Journal of Marriage and Family showed that parents who prioritized self-care reported lower parenting stress and higher relationship satisfaction (Nelson et al., 2014).

c) Mid-life: Address changing physical needs and career stressors. Research in the Journal of Occupational Health Psychology found that mid-life adults who engaged in regular self-care reported higher job satisfaction and lower burnout (Sonnentag, 2012).

d) Retirement: Focus on maintaining purpose and social connections. A study in The Journals of Gerontology found that retirees who engaged in purposeful activities reported higher levels of well-being (Lum & Lightfoot, 2005).

e) Later life: Emphasize practices that support cognitive health and physical mobility. Research in the Journal of the American Geriatrics Society demonstrated that older adults who engaged in regular physical and mental activities had a lower risk of cognitive decline (Wang et al., 2013).

Dr. Laura Carstensen, Professor of Psychology at Stanford University, emphasizes: "As we age, our time horizons shorten, and our goals change. Self-care practices should shift to align with these changing perspectives" (Carstensen, 2006).

1. **Tracking progress and adjusting your rituals**

Regularly monitoring and adjusting self-care practices ensures their continued effectiveness and relevance.

Dr. BJ Fogg, founder of the Behavior Design Lab at Stanford University, states: "For behavior change to stick, people need to feel successful. Tracking progress provides that sense of accomplishment" (Fogg, 2019).

Key strategies for tracking progress and adjusting rituals include:

a) Journaling: Keep a self-care journal to track practices and their effects. A study in Advances in Psychiatric Treatment found that reflective writing improved insight and promoted positive behavioral change (Bolton et al., 2004).

b) Use of technology: Utilize apps or wearable devices to monitor self-care activities and their impacts. Research in the Journal of Medical Internet Research showed that digital self-tracking tools can increase engagement with health-promoting behaviors (Patel et al., 2015).

c) Regular self-assessments: Conduct periodic reviews of well-being and stress levels. A study in Assessment found that regular self-assessment was associated with increased self-awareness and improved mental health outcomes (Trapnell & Campbell, 1999).

d) Seeking feedback: Engage with trusted friends, family, or professionals for external perspectives. Research in the Journal of Applied Psychology demonstrated that seeking feedback was associated with improved performance and personal growth (Ashford & Cummings, 1983).

e) Experimentation: Be willing to try new self-care practices and adjust existing ones. A study in Personality and Social Psychology Bulletin found that individuals who approached personal growth with a growth mindset showed greater improvement over time (Dweck, 2006).

Dr. Angela Duckworth, Professor of Psychology at the University of Pennsylvania, emphasizes: "The key to long-term success is having the flexibility to learn and adapt. This applies to self-care as much as any other area of life" (Duckworth, 2016).

Incorporating these strategies for customizing your self-care revolution – creating a personalized plan, overcoming obstacles, adapting practices for different life stages, and tracking progress – can significantly enhance the effectiveness and sustainability of your self-care practice. Remember that self-care is a dynamic process that requires ongoing attention and adjustment. By regularly reflecting on and refining your self-care practices, you can ensure that they continue to support your well-being throughout the various phases and challenges of life. The ultimate goal is to develop a flexible, personalized approach to self-care that evolves with you, providing consistent support for your physical, emotional, and mental health.

Conclusion

1. Reflecting on your self-care journey

Reflection is a crucial component of any personal growth journey, including the development of a robust self-care practice. It allows for deeper understanding, integration of lessons learned, and recognition of progress made.

Dr. Jennifer Guttman, clinical psychologist and author, states: "Reflection is not just about looking back, but about making meaning of our experiences and using that insight to inform our future actions" (Guttman, 2020).

Key aspects of reflecting on your self-care journey include:

a) Acknowledging progress: Recognize and celebrate the positive changes you've made. Research in the Journal of Personality and Social Psychology found that acknowledging progress increases motivation and commitment to goals (Fishbach & Dhar, 2005).

b) Identifying challenges: Reflect on obstacles encountered and strategies used to overcome them. A study in the Journal of Applied Psychology demonstrated that reflecting on challenges and solutions improved problem-solving skills and resilience (Ellis et al., 2014).

c) Assessing impact: Consider how your self-care practices have affected various aspects of your life. Research in the Journal of Happiness Studies showed that regular reflection on personal growth experiences enhanced well-being and life satisfaction (Roepke et al., 2013).

d) Recognizing patterns: Look for recurring themes or patterns in your self-care journey. A study in Psychological Science found that identifying patterns in behavior and experiences can lead to more effective personal change strategies (Gilovich & Ross, 2015).

e) Setting future intentions: Use insights from reflection to inform future self-care goals. Research in the European Journal of Social Psychology demonstrated that setting intentions based on past experiences increased the likelihood of achieving goals (Gollwitzer & Sheeran, 2006).

Dr. Kristin Neff, pioneer in self-compassion research, emphasizes: "Reflection on our self-care journey should be done with kindness and compassion. It's not about judgment, but about learning and growth" (Neff, 2011).

1. **The ripple effect: How your self-care impacts others**

Self-care is not just a personal practice; its effects extend beyond the individual, influencing relationships, work environments, and communities.

Dr. Emma Seppälä, Science Director of Stanford University's Center for Compassion and Altruism Research and Education, states: "When we take care of ourselves, we are better able to care for others. Self-care is, in fact, an act of altruism" (Seppälä, 2016).

Key aspects of the ripple effect of self-care include:

a) Improved relationships: When we're well-cared for, we have more to give in our relationships. A study in the Journal of Social and Personal Relationships found that individuals who practiced self-care reported higher relationship satisfaction and were perceived as more supportive by their partners (Neff & Beretvas, 2013).

b) Enhanced work performance: Self-care can lead to increased productivity and job satisfaction. Research in the Journal of Occupational

Health Psychology demonstrated that employees who engaged in regular self-care practices showed higher levels of job performance and lower levels of burnout (Sonnentag, 2003).

c) Modeling healthy behaviors: Our self-care practices can inspire others to prioritize their well-being. A study in Health Education & Behavior found that individuals were more likely to engage in health-promoting behaviors when they observed these behaviors in others (Umberson et al., 2010).

d) Community well-being: Personal self-care can contribute to broader community health. Research in the American Journal of Public Health showed that communities with higher levels of individual well-being had better overall public health outcomes (Keyes & Simoes, 2012).

e) Generational impact: Self-care practices can be passed down, influencing future generations. A study in Developmental Psychology found that parental self-care behaviors significantly influenced their children's health behaviors in adulthood (Wickrama et al., 1999).

Dr. Brené Brown, research professor at the University of Houston, emphasizes: "When we fill our own cups, we have more to pour into others. Self-care is not selfish; it's necessary for our collective well-being" (Brown, 2018).

1. Continuing to evolve your self-care practice

Self-care is not a destination but an ongoing journey that requires continuous adaptation and growth.

Dr. Shauna Shapiro, clinical psychologist and author, states: "Self-care is a practice, not a perfect. It's about continually showing up for ourselves with kindness and curiosity" (Shapiro, 2020).

Key strategies for continuing to evolve your self-care practice include:

a) Regular reassessment: Periodically evaluate the effectiveness of your self-care strategies. A study in the Journal of Counseling Psychology found that regular reassessment of coping strategies led to more effective stress management over time (Folkman & Moskowitz, 2004).

b) Exploring new practices: Be open to trying new self-care techniques. Research in Frontiers in Psychology showed that engaging in novel experiences can enhance well-being and personal growth (Kashdan & Silvia, 2009).

c) Deepening existing practices: Look for ways to deepen your understanding and implementation of current self-care rituals. A study in Mindfulness demonstrated that deepening mindfulness practices over time led to increased psychological well-being (Carmody & Baer, 2008).

d) Adapting to life changes: Adjust your self-care practice as your life circumstances evolve. Research in the Annual Review of Psychology highlighted the importance of flexible coping strategies in maintaining well-being across the lifespan (Bonanno & Burton, 2013).

e) Integrating research and personal experience: Stay informed about new self-care research while honoring your personal experiences. A study in the Journal of Clinical Psychology found that integrating empirical evidence with personal insights led to more effective therapeutic practices, a principle that can be applied to self-care (Castonguay et al., 2006).

Dr. Rick Hanson, psychologist and Senior Fellow of the Greater Good Science Center at UC Berkeley, emphasizes: "The brain is like Velcro for negative experiences but Teflon for positive ones. We need to consciously internalize positive experiences through self-care to build resilience over time" (Hanson, 2013).

In conclusion, the journey of self-care is deeply personal yet universally impactful. By reflecting on our progress, recognizing the far-reaching effects of our self-care, and committing to the ongoing evolution of our practices, we not only enhance our own well-being but contribute to the betterment of our relationships, communities, and even future generations. Remember that self-care is not a luxury or a selfish act, but a fundamental responsibility we have to ourselves and those around us. As you continue on your self-care journey, approach it with curiosity, compassion, and a willingness to grow and adapt. Your commitment to self-care is a powerful force for positive change, both in your own life and in the world around you.

Resources

1. **Recommended apps for tracking self-care**

Mobile applications can be valuable tools for monitoring and maintaining self-care practices. Here are some research-backed and professionally recommended apps:

a) **Headspace:** A meditation and mindfulness app. Research published in the Journal of Medical Internet Research found that using Headspace for 10 days resulted in reduced stress and increased compassion (Howells et al., 2016).

b) **Calm:** Another popular meditation and sleep app. A study in the Journal of Clinical Sleep Medicine showed that using Calm improved sleep outcomes in adults with insomnia (Huberty et al., 2021).

c) **Moodfit:** A mood tracking and mental health app. While not specifically studied, mood tracking apps have been shown to be effective tools for self-monitoring in mental health care (Bakker & Rickard, 2018).

d) **Daylio:** A mood and activity diary. Journaling apps like Daylio can help in identifying patterns in mood and behavior, which is crucial for effective self-care (Rickard et al., 2016).

e) **Fitbit:** For tracking physical activity and sleep. A systematic review in JMIR mHealth and uHealth found that Fitbit devices are valid and reliable for measuring steps and sleep duration (Feehan et al., 2018).

f) **MyFitnessPal:** For nutrition tracking. Research in the Journal of

Medical Internet Research found that consistent use of MyFitnessPal was associated with greater weight loss (Jacobs et al., 2017).

Dr. John Torous, Director of the Digital Psychiatry Division at Beth Israel Deaconess Medical Center, emphasizes: "While apps can be useful tools for self-care, it's important to choose evidence-based apps and to use them as part of a broader self-care strategy, not as a replacement for professional care when needed" (Torous et al., 2018).

1. **Books and websites for further reading**

For those looking to deepen their understanding of self-care, the following books and websites come highly recommended by professionals in the field:

Books:

a) **"The Self-Care Project"** by Jayne Hardy - Offers practical strategies for incorporating self-care into daily life.

b) **"Self-Compassion"** The Proven Power of Being Kind to Yourself" by Dr. Kristin Neff - Explores the concept of self-compassion as a foundation for self-care.

c) **"Burnout"** The Secret to Unlocking the Stress Cycle" by Emily Nagoski and Amelia Nagoski - Provides science-based strategies for managing stress and preventing burnout.

d) **"The Body Keeps the Score"** by Bessel van der Kolk - Discusses the impact of trauma on the body and mind, and offers approaches for healing.

e) **"Atomic Habits"** by James Clear - While not specifically about self-care, this book provides valuable insights into forming and maintaining positive habits.

Websites:

a) **Psychology Today** (www.psychologytoday.com) - Offers a wealth of articles on mental health and self-care topics.

b) **Greater Good Science Center** (greatergood.berkeley.edu) - Provides science-based insights for a meaningful life.

c) **National Institute of Mental Health** (www.nimh.nih.gov) - Offers evidence-based information on mental health and self-care.

d) **Mindful** (www.mindful.org) - Provides resources and articles on mindfulness and meditation.

Dr. Alex Korb, neuroscientist and author, states: "Reading about self-care can provide new perspectives and strategies. However, the key is to not just consume information, but to apply it in your daily life" (Korb, 2015).

1. **Self-care assessment tools**

Self-care assessment tools can help individuals identify areas of strength and potential improvement in their self-care practices. Here are some validated tools recommended by professionals:

a) **The Self-Care Assessment Worksheet (SCAW):** Developed by Saakvitne and Pearlman, this comprehensive tool assesses physical, psychological, emotional, spiritual, and professional self-care practices (Saakvitne & Pearlman, 1996).

b) **The Professional Quality of Life Scale (ProQOL):** While designed for professionals in helping roles, this scale can be useful for anyone to assess compassion satisfaction, burnout, and secondary traumatic stress (Stamm, 2010).

c) **The Perceived Stress Scale (PSS):** This widely used psychological instrument measures the degree to which situations in one's life are appraised as stressful (Cohen et al., 1983).

d) **The Self-Compassion Scale (SCS):** Developed by Dr. Kristin Neff, this scale measures self-compassion, a key component of effective self-care (Neff, 2003).

e) **The Wellness Assessment:** Created by the National Wellness

Institute, this tool assesses six dimensions of wellness: physical, emotional, spiritual, intellectual, social, and occupational (Hettler, 1976).

Dr. Catherine Cook-Cottone, Professor of Counseling, School, and Educational Psychology at the University at Buffalo, emphasizes: "Self-assessment tools are not diagnostic instruments, but rather starting points for reflection and discussion. They can help guide your self-care journey by highlighting areas that may need more attention" (Cook-Cottone, 2015).

14

Sources Chapter 2

Cited Sources:

Elrod, H. (2012). The Miracle Morning: The Not-So-Obvious Secret Guaranteed to Transform Your Life (Before 8AM). Hal Elrod International.

Fenn, A. (2022). The Brain Health Kitchen: Preventing Alzheimer's Through Food. Artisan.

Galioto, R., & Spitznagel, M. B. (2021). The Effects of Breakfast and Breakfast Composition on Cognition in Adults. Nutrients, 13(4), 1324.

Harvey, A. G., et al. (2016). Treating Sleep Problems: A Transdiagnostic Approach. Guilford Press.

Hafeez, S. (2020). The Importance of Routines, According to Psychologists. Verywell Mind.

Kitsantas, A., et al. (2019). The Role of Self-Regulated Strategies and Goal Orientation in Predicting Achievement of Elementary School Children. International Electronic Journal of Elementary Education, 4(1), 65-81.

Smeets, E., et al. (2020). Start with a Smile: Morning Positive Mood and Daily Mental Health. Mindfulness, 11, 2519–2531.

Thirthalli, J., et al. (2013). Cortisol and antidepressant effects of yoga. Indian Journal of Psychiatry, 55(Suppl 3), S405–S408.

Wheeler, M. J., et al. (2019). Distinct effects of acute exercise and breaks in sitting on working memory and executive function in older adults: a three-arm, randomised cross-over trial to evaluate the effects of exercise with and without breaks in sitting on cognition. British Journal of Sports Medicine, 53(22), 1414-1422.

15

Sources Chapter 3:

Cited Sources:

Armstrong, L. E., et al. (2012). Mild dehydration affects mood in healthy young women. The Journal of Nutrition, 142(2), 382-388.

Arch, J. J., et al. (2016). Mindfulness-based interventions for obesity-related eating behaviours: A literature review. Obesity Reviews, 17(5), 453-461.

Brown, B. (2010). The gifts of imperfection: Let go of who you think you're supposed to be and embrace who you are. Hazelden Publishing.

Hunter, M. R., et al. (2019). Urban nature experiences reduce stress in the context of daily life based on salivary biomarkers. Frontiers in Psychology, 10, 722.

Kim, S., et al. (2017). Daily micro-breaks and job performance: General work engagement as a cross-level moderator. Journal of Applied Psychology, 102(12), 1702-1713.

Kim, S., et al. (2018). Workplace flexibility and employee well-being: Propensity score analysis. Journal of Organizational Behavior, 39(3), 369-385.

Kossek, E. E., et al. (2012). Work-nonwork boundary management profiles: A person-centered approach. Journal of Vocational Behavior, 81(1), 112-128.

Langer, E. J. (2014). Mindfulness. Da Capo Press.

Lomas, T., et al. (2017). A systematic review of the impact of mindfulness on the well-being of healthcare professionals. Journal of Clinical Psychology, 73(7), 808-824.

Lovato, N., & Lack, L. (2010). The effects of napping on cognitive functioning. Progress in Brain Research, 185, 155-166.

Masento, N. A., et al. (2014). Effects of hydration status on cognitive performance and mood. British Journal of Nutrition, 111(10), 1841-1852.

Pross, N., et al. (2013). Effects of changes in water intake on mood of high and low drinkers. PloS One, 8(4), e59966.

Pross, N., et al. (2014). Influence of progressive fluid restriction on mood and physiological markers of dehydration in women. British Journal of Nutrition, 111(2), 313-321.

Sonnentag, S., et al. (2017). Recovery from job stress: The stressor-detachment model as an integrative framework. Journal of Organizational Behavior, 38(6), 792-812.

Thøgersen-Ntoumani, C., et al. (2015). Changes in work affect in response to lunchtime walking in previously physically inactive employees: A randomized trial. Scandinavian Journal of Medicine & Science in Sports, 25(6), 778-787.

16

Sources Chapter 4:

Cited Sources:

Black, D. S., et al. (2015). Mindfulness meditation and improvement in sleep quality and daytime impairment among older adults with sleep disturbances: A randomized clinical trial. JAMA Internal Medicine, 175(4), 494-501.

Boubekri, M., et al. (2014). Impact of windows and daylight exposure on overall health and sleep quality of office workers: A case-control pilot study. Journal of Clinical Sleep Medicine, 10(6), 603-611.

Chen, S. F., et al. (2018). Effects of non-pharmacological interventions on sleep quality during pregnancy: A systematic review and meta-analysis. Sleep Medicine Reviews, 44, 35-47.

Chellappa, S. L., et al. (2013). Non-visual effects of light on melatonin, alertness and cognitive performance: Can blue-enriched light keep us alert? PloS One, 8(10), e76707.

Hertenstein, E., et al. (2019). Insomnia as a predictor of mental disorders: A systematic review and meta-analysis. Sleep Medicine Reviews, 43, 96-105.

Jacobson, B. H., et al. (2008). Effect of prescribed sleep surfaces on back pain and sleep quality in patients diagnosed with low back and shoulder pain. Applied Ergonomics, 39(2), 247-254.

Khalsa, S. B. S. (2012). Yoga for psychiatry and mental health: An ancient practice with modern relevance. Indian Journal of Psychiatry, 54(3), 203-204.

Lin, H. H., et al. (2011). Effect of kiwifruit consumption on sleep quality in adults with sleep problems. Asia Pacific Journal of Clinical Nutrition, 20(2), 169-174.

Lillehei, A. S., et al. (2015). Effect of inhaled lavender and sleep hygiene on self-reported sleep issues: A randomized controlled trial. Journal of Alternative and Complementary Medicine, 21(7), 430-438.

Lovato, N., et al. (2019). Cognitive and behavioral therapies in the treatment of insomnia: A meta-analysis. Health Psychology Review, 13(1), 73-90.

Meerlo, P., et al. (2008). Restricted and disrupted sleep: Effects on autonomic function, neuroendocrine stress systems and stress responsivity. Sleep Medicine Reviews, 12(3), 197-210.

Messineo, L., et al. (2017). Broadband sound administration improves sleep onset latency in healthy subjects in a model of transient insomnia. Frontiers in Neurology, 8, 718.

Mishra, A. K., et al. (2018). Window/door opening-mediated bedroom ventilation and its impact on sleep quality of healthy, young adults. Indoor Air, 28(2), 339-351.

Neuendorf, R., et al. (2015). The effects of mind-body interventions on sleep quality: A systematic review. Evidence-Based Complementary and Alternative Medicine, 2015, 902708.

Obayashi, K., et al. (2013). Exposure to light at night, nocturnal urinary melatonin excretion, and obesity/dyslipidemia in the elderly: A cross-sectional analysis of the HEIJO-KYO study. The Journal of Clinical Endocrinology & Metabolism, 98(1), 337-344.

Rani, K., et al. (2012). Impact of Yoga Nidra on psychological general wellbeing in patients with menstrual irregularities: A randomized controlled trial. International Journal of Yoga, 5(1), 52-56.

Roster, C. A., et al. (2016). The role of mindfulness in achieving life balance. Journal of Consumer Affairs, 50(1), 128-152.

Scullin, M. K., et al. (2018). The effects of bedtime writing on difficulty falling asleep: A polysomnographic study comparing to-do lists and completed activity lists. Journal of Experimental Psychology: General, 147(1), 139-146.

Walker, M. P. (2017). Why we sleep: Unlocking the power of sleep and dreams. Scribner.

Wang, C. F., et al. (2014). The effect of music in aromatherapy on pain responses of grad school students with moderate anxiety: A small-scale clinical study. International Journal of Nursing Practice, 20(6), 638-646.

Weil, A. (2016). Breathing: The master key to self-healing. Sounds True.

Williamson, A. M., & Feyer, A. M. (2000). Moderate sleep deprivation produces impairments in cognitive and motor performance equivalent to legally prescribed levels of alcohol intoxication. Occupational and Environmental Medicine, 57(10), 649-655.

Yoo, S. S., et al. (2007). The human emotional brain without sleep—a prefrontal amygdala disconnect. Current Biology, 17(20), R877-R878.

17

Sources Chapter 5:

Cited Sources:

Abbing, A., et al. (2018). The effectiveness of art therapy for anxiety in adults: A systematic review of randomised and non-randomised controlled trials. PloS One, 13(12), e0208716.

Bolton, G., et al. (2004). Writing cures: An introductory handbook of writing in counselling and psychotherapy. Routledge.

Bradt, J., et al. (2015). Music interventions for improving psychological and physical outcomes in cancer patients. Cochrane Database of Systematic Reviews, (8), CD006911.

Breines, J. G., & Chen, S. (2012). Self-compassion increases self-improvement motivation. Personality and Social Psychology Bulletin, 38(9), 1133-1143.

Brown, B. (2010). The gifts of imperfection: Let go of who you think you're supposed to be and embrace who you are. Hazelden Publishing.

Cheng, S. T., et al. (2022). Gratitude and depression: The role of positive reframing and positive emotion. Journal of Happiness Studies, 23(2), 569-586.

Emmons, R. A., & McCullough, M. E. (2003). Counting blessings versus burdens: An experimental investigation of gratitude and subjective well-being in daily life. Journal of Personality and Social Psychology, 84(2), 377-389.

Frattaroli, J. (2006). Experimental disclosure and its moderators: A meta-analysis. Psychological Bulletin, 132(6), 823-865.

Germer, C. K. (2009). The mindful path to self-compassion: Freeing yourself from destructive thoughts and emotions. Guilford Press.

Kini, P., et al. (2016). The effects of gratitude expression on neural activity. NeuroImage, 128, 1-10.

Klein, K., & Boals, A. (2001). Expressive writing can increase working memory capacity. Journal of Experimental Psychology: General, 130(3), 520-533.

Korb, A. (2015). The upward spiral: Using neuroscience to reverse the course of depression, one small change at a time. New Harbinger Publications.

Leary, M. R., et al. (2007). Self-compassion and reactions to unpleasant self-relevant events: The implications of treating oneself kindly. Journal of Personality and Social Psychology, 92(5), 887-904.

Levine, P. A. (2010). In an unspoken voice: How the body releases trauma and restores goodness. North Atlantic Books.

Lieberman, M. D., et al. (2007). Putting feelings into words: Affect labeling disrupts amygdala activity in response to affective stimuli. Psychological Science, 18(5), 421-428.

Malchiodi, C. A. (2011). Handbook of art therapy. Guilford Press.

Miller, L. (2015). The spiritual child: The new science on parenting for health and lifelong thriving. St. Martin's Press.

Neff, K. D. (2003). The development and validation of a scale to measure self-compassion. Self and Identity, 2(3), 223-250.

Neff, K. D. (2011). Self-compassion, self-esteem, and well-being. Social and Personality Psychology Compass, 5(1), 1-12.

Pelletier, C. L. (2004). The effect of music on decreasing arousal due to stress: A meta-analysis. Journal of Music Therapy, 41(3), 192-214.

Pennebaker, J. W. (1997). Writing about emotional experiences as a therapeutic process. Psychological Science, 8(3), 162-166.

Pennebaker, J. W., & Francis, M. E. (1996). Cognitive, emotional, and language processes in disclosure. Cognition & Emotion, 10(6), 601-626.

Tang, Y. Y., et al. (2015). The neuroscience of mindfulness meditation. Nature Reviews Neuroscience, 16(4), 213-225.

Turk, F., & Waller, G. (2020). Is self-compassion relevant to the pathology and treatment of eating and body image concerns? A systematic review and meta-analysis. Clinical Psychology Review, 79, 101856.

Wilson, A. C., et al. (2019). Effectiveness of self-compassion related therapies: A systematic review and meta-analysis. Mindfulness, 10(6), 979-995.

18

Sources Chapter 7:

Cited Sources:

Brown, B. (2010). The gifts of imperfection: Let go of who you think you're supposed to be and embrace who you are. Hazelden Publishing.

Cain, S. (2012). Quiet: The power of introverts in a world that can't stop talking. Crown Publishers.

Cacioppo, J. T., Hughes, M. E., Waite, L. J., Hawkley, L. C., & Thisted, R. A. (2006). Loneliness as a specific risk factor for depressive symptoms: Cross-sectional and longitudinal analyses. Psychology and Aging, 21(1), 140-151.

Cloud, H., & Townsend, J. (1992). Boundaries: When to say yes, how to say no to take control of your life. Zondervan.

Corrigan, P. W., Kosyluk, K. A., & Rüsch, N. (2013). Reducing self-stigma by coming out proud. American Journal of Public Health, 103(5), 794-800.

Goncalo, J. A., & Staw, B. M. (2006). Individualism–collectivism and group creativity. Organizational Behavior and Human Decision Processes, 100(1), 96-109.

Haslam, C., Cruwys, T., Haslam, S. A., Dingle, G., & Chang, M. X. L.

(2016). Groups 4 Health: Evidence that a social-identity intervention that builds and strengthens social group membership improves mental health. Journal of Affective Disorders, 194, 188-195.

Holt-Lunstad, J., Smith, T. B., & Layton, J. B. (2010). Social relationships and mortality risk: A meta-analytic review. PLoS Medicine, 7(7), e1000316.

Knapp, J. L., Holliday, C. E., & Wilson, V. L. (2017). The relationship between couple's attachment styles and their marital satisfaction. Family Journal, 25(4), 375-385.

Kossek, E. E., Ruderman, M. N., Braddy, P. W., & Hannum, K. M. (2012). Work–nonwork boundary management profiles: A person-centered approach. Journal of Vocational Behavior, 81(1), 112-128.

Larson, R. W., & Lee, M. (1996). The capacity to be alone as a stress buffer. The Journal of Social Psychology, 136(1), 5-16.

Lee, J., Lim, N., Yang, E., & Lee, S. M. (2011). Antecedents and consequences of three dimensions of burnout in psychotherapists: A meta-analysis. Professional Psychology: Research and Practice, 42(3), 252-258.

Long, C. R., Seburn, M., Averill, J. R., & More, T. A. (2003). Solitude experiences: Varieties, settings, and individual differences. Personality and Social Psychology Bulletin, 29(5), 578-583.

Marano, H. E. (2003). What is solitude? Psychology Today, 36(4), 70-76.

Nguyen, T. V. T., Ryan, R. M., & Deci, E. L. (2018). Solitude as an approach to affective self-regulation. Personality and Social Psychology Bulletin, 44(1), 92-106.

Pargament, K. I. (2007). Spiritually integrated psychotherapy: Understanding and addressing the sacred. Guilford Press.

Pfeiffer, P. N., Heisler, M., Piette, J. D., Rogers, M. A., & Valenstein, M. (2011). Efficacy of peer support interventions for depression: A meta-analysis. General Hospital Psychiatry, 33(1), 29-36.

Seppälä, E. M. (2014). Connectedness & health: The science of social connection. Stanford Medicine.

Uchino, B. N., Cacioppo, J. T., & Kiecolt-Glaser, J. K. (1996). The relationship between social support and physiological processes: A review with emphasis on underlying mechanisms and implications for health. Psychological Bulletin, 119(3), 488-531.

Ussher, J., Kirsten, L., Butow, P., & Sandoval, M. (2006). What do cancer support groups provide which other supportive relationships do not? The experience of peer support groups for people with cancer. Social Science & Medicine, 62(10), 2565-2576.

Waldinger, R. J. (2015). What makes a good life? Lessons from the longest study on happiness. TED Talk.

Yalom, I. D. (1995). The theory and practice of group psychotherapy. Basic Books.

Zunzunegui, M. V., Alvarado, B. E., Del Ser, T., & Otero, A. (2003). Social networks, social integration, and social engagement determine cognitive decline in community-dwelling Spanish older adults. The Journals of Gerontology Series B: Psychological Sciences and Social Sciences, 58(2), S93-S100.

19

Sources Chapter 8:

Cited Sources:

Atchley, R. A., & Strayer, D. L. (2017). Small screen use and driving safety. Pediatrics, 140(Supplement 2), S107-S111.

Barber, L. K., & Santuzzi, A. M. (2015). Please respond ASAP: Workplace telepressure and employee recovery. Journal of Occupational Health Psychology, 20(2), 172-189.

Burke, M., & Kraut, R. E. (2016). The relationship between Facebook use and well-being depends on communication type and tie strength. Journal of Computer-Mediated Communication, 21(4), 265-281.

Chang, A. M., Aeschbach, D., Duffy, J. F., & Czeisler, C. A. (2015). Evening use of light-emitting eReaders negatively affects sleep, circadian timing, and next-morning alertness. Proceedings of the National Academy of Sciences, 112(4), 1232-1237.

Dodgen-Magee, D. (2018). Deviced! Balancing life and technology in a digital world. Rowman & Littlefield.

Hunt, M. G., Marx, R., Lipson, C., & Young, J. (2018). No more FOMO: Limiting social media decreases loneliness and depression. Journal of Social and Clinical Psychology, 37(10), 751-768.

Kramer, A. D., Guillory, J. E., & Hancock, J. T. (2014). Experimental evidence of massive-scale emotional contagion through social networks. Proceedings of the National Academy of Sciences, 111(24), 8788-8790.

Li, J., Pearce, P. L., & Low, D. (2018). Media representation of digital-free tourism: A critical discourse analysis. Tourism Management, 69, 317-329.

Newport, C. (2019). Digital minimalism: Choosing a focused life in a noisy world. Portfolio.

Ophir, E., Nass, C., & Wagner, A. D. (2009). Cognitive control in media multitaskers. Proceedings of the National Academy of Sciences, 106(37), 15583-15587.

Panger, G. (2018). Reassessing the Facebook experiment: Critical thinking about the validity of Big Data research. Information, Communication & Society, 21(2), 224-238.

Pang, A. S. K. (2013). The distraction addiction: Getting the information you need and the communication you want, without enraging your family, annoying your colleagues, and destroying your soul. Little, Brown and Company.

Perrault, A. A., Bayer, L., Peuvrier, M., Afyouni, A., Ghisletta, P., Brockmann, C., ... & Sterpenich, V. (2019). Reducing the use of screen electronic devices in the evening is associated with improved sleep and daytime vigilance in adolescents. Sleep, 42(9), zsz125.

Primack, B. A., Shensa, A., Sidani, J. E., Whaite, E. O., Lin, L. Y., Rosen, D., ... & Miller, E. (2017). Social media use and perceived social isolation among young adults in the US. American Journal of Preventive Medicine, 53(1), 1-8.

Przybylski, A. K., & Weinstein, N. (2013). Can you connect with me now? How the presence of mobile communication technology influences face-to-face conversation quality. Journal of Social and Personal Relationships, 30(3), 237-246.

Rodríguez-García, A. M., Moreno-Guerrero, A. J., & López Belmonte,

J. (2020). Nomophobia: An individual's growing fear of being without a smartphone—A systematic literature review. International Journal of Environmental Research and Public Health, 17(2), 580.

Rosen, L. D. (2012). iDisorder: Understanding our obsession with technology and overcoming its hold on us. Palgrave Macmillan.

Salo, M., Pirkkalainen, H., & Koskelainen, T. (2019). Technostress and social networking services: Explaining users' concentration, sleep, identity, and social relation problems. Information Systems Journal, 29(2), 408-435.

Shen, C., Wang, M. P., Chu, J. T., Wan, A., Viswanath, K., Chan, S. S. C., & Lam, T. H. (2017). Health app possession among smartphone or tablet owners in Hong Kong: Population-based survey. JMIR mHealth and uHealth, 5(6), e77.

Steers, M. L. N., Wickham, R. E., & Acitelli, L. K. (2014). Seeing everyone else's highlight reels: How Facebook usage is linked to depressive symptoms. Journal of Social and Clinical Psychology, 33(8), 701-731.

Sutton, T. (2017). Disconnect to reconnect: The food/technology metaphor in digital detoxing. First Monday, 22(6).

Twenge, J. M. (2017). iGen: Why today's super-connected kids are growing up less rebellious, more tolerant, less happy—and completely unprepared for adulthood—and what that means for the rest of us. Atria Books.

Vanman, E. J., Baker, R., & Tobin, S. J. (2018). The burden of online friends: The effects of giving up Facebook on stress and well-being. The Journal of Social Psychology, 158(4), 496-507.

Verduyn, P., Ybarra, O., Résibois, M., Jonides, J., & Kross, E. (2017). Do social network sites enhance or undermine subjective well-being? A critical review. Social Issues and Policy Review, 11(1), 274-302.

Vogel, E. A., Rose, J. P., Roberts, L. R., & Eckles, K. (2020). Social comparison, social media, and self-esteem. Psychology of Popular Media, 3(3), 206-217.

20

Sources Chapter 9:

Cited Sources:

Atchley, R. A., Strayer, D. L., & Atchley, P. (2012). Creativity in the wild: Improving creative reasoning through immersion in natural settings. PloS One, 7(12), e51474.

Augustin, S. (2009). Place advantage: Applied psychology for interior architecture. John Wiley & Sons.

Berman, M. G., Jonides, J., & Kaplan, S. (2008). The cognitive benefits of interacting with nature. Psychological Science, 19(12), 1207–1212.

Capaldi, C. A., Dopko, R. L., & Zelenski, J. M. (2014). The relationship between nature connectedness and happiness: A meta-analysis. Frontiers in Psychology, 5, 976.

Clayton, S. D. (2012). The Oxford handbook of environmental and conservation psychology. Oxford University Press.

Dinnie, E., Brown, K. M., & Morris, S. (2013). Community, cooperation and conflict: Negotiating the social well-being benefits of urban greenspace experiences. Landscape and Urban Planning, 112, 1–9.

Elliot, A. J. (2015). Color and psychological functioning: A review of theoretical and empirical work. Frontiers in Psychology, 6, 368.

Fjeld, T. (2000). The effect of interior planting on health and discomfort among workers and school children. HortTechnology, 10(1), 46-52.

Helm, S. V., Pollitt, A., Barnett, M. A., Curran, M. A., & Craig, Z. R. (2018). Differentiating environmental concern in the context of psychological adaptation to climate change. Global Environmental Change, 48, 158-167.

Hunter, M. R., Gillespie, B. W., & Chen, S. Y. P. (2019). Urban nature experiences reduce stress in the context of daily life based on salivary biomarkers. Frontiers in Psychology, 10, 722.

Israel, T. (2003). Some place like home: Using design psychology to create ideal places. Wiley-Academy.

Karakolis, T., & Callaghan, J. P. (2014). The impact of sit–stand office workstations on worker discomfort and productivity: A review. Applied Ergonomics, 45(3), 799-806.

Koselka, E. P., Weidner, L. C., Minasov, A., Berman, M. G., Leonard, W. R., Santoso, M. V., ... & Horton, T. H. (2021). Walking green: Developing an evidence base for nature prescriptions. International Journal of Environmental Research and Public Health, 18(9), 4338.

Kuo, M. (2015). How might contact with nature promote human health? Promising mechanisms and a possible central pathway. Frontiers in Psychology, 6, 1093.

Lee, M. S., Lee, J., Park, B. J., & Miyazaki, Y. (2015). Interaction with indoor plants may reduce psychological and physiological stress by suppressing autonomic nervous system activity in young adults: A randomized crossover study. Journal of Physiological Anthropology, 34(1), 21.

Lohr, V. I. (2010). What are the benefits of plants indoors and why do we respond positively to them? Acta Horticulturae, 881, 675-682.

Martin, A., Goryakin, Y., & Suhrcke, M. (2014). Does active commuting improve psychological wellbeing? Longitudinal evidence from eighteen waves of the British Household Panel Survey. Preventive Medicine, 69, 296-303.

Nisbet, E. K., Zelenski, J. M., & Murphy, S. A. (2011). Happiness is in our nature: Exploring nature relatedness as a contributor to subjective well-being. Journal of Happiness Studies, 12(2), 303-322.

Pahl, S., Sheppard, S., Boomsma, C., & Groves, C. (2017). Perceptions of time in relation to climate change. Wiley Interdisciplinary Reviews: Climate Change, 8(5), e459.

Raanaas, R. K., Evensen, K. H., Rich, D., Sjøstrøm, G., & Patil, G. (2011). Benefits of indoor plants on attention capacity in an office setting. Journal of Environmental Psychology, 31(1), 99-105.

Roster, C. A., Ferrari, J. R., & Jurkat, M. P. (2016). The dark side of home: Assessing possession 'clutter' on subjective well-being. Journal of Environmental Psychology, 46, 32-41.

Shibata, S., & Suzuki, N. (2004). Effects of an indoor plant on creative task performance and mood. Scandinavian Journal of Psychology, 45(5), 373-381.

Toyoda, M., Yokota, Y., & Rodiek, S. (2020). Gardening may reduce blood pressure in the elderly: A pilot randomized controlled trial. Complementary Therapies in Medicine, 50, 102401.

Venhoeven, L. A., Bolderdijk, J. W., & Steg, L. (2013). Explaining the paradox: How pro-environmental behaviour can both thwart and foster well-being. Sustainability, 5(4), 1372-1386.

Wells, M. M. (2000). Office clutter or meaningful personal displays: The role of office personalization in employee and organizational well-being. Journal of Environmental Psychology, 20(3), 239-255.

White, M. P., Alcock, I., Grellier, J., Wheeler, B. W., Hartig, T., Warber, S. L., ... & Fleming, L. E. (2019). Spending at least 120 minutes a week in nature is associated with good health and wellbeing. Scientific Reports, 9(1), 7730.

Wolverton, B. C., Johnson, A., & Bounds, K. (1989). Interior landscape plants for indoor air pollution abatement. NASA Technical Report.

21

Sources Chapter 10:

Cited Sources:

Black, D. S., O'Reilly, G. A., Olmstead, R., Breen, E. C., & Irwin, M. R. (2015). Mindfulness meditation and improvement in sleep quality and daytime impairment among older adults with sleep disturbances: A randomized clinical trial. JAMA Internal Medicine, 175(4), 494-501.

Carmody, J., & Baer, R. A. (2008). Relationships between mindfulness practice and levels of mindfulness, medical and psychological symptoms and well-being in a mindfulness-based stress reduction program. Journal of Behavioral Medicine, 31(1), 23-33.

Castonguay, L. G., Boswell, J. F., Constantino, M. J., Goldfried, M. R., & Hill, C. E. (2006). Training implications of harmful effects of psychological treatments. American Psychologist, 61(2), 157-168.

Creswell, J. D., Taren, A. A., Lindsay, E. K., Greco, C. M., Gianaros, P. J., Fairgrieve, A., ... & Ferris, J. L. (2016). Alterations in resting-state functional connectivity link mindfulness meditation with reduced interleukin-6: A randomized controlled trial. Biological Psychiatry, 80(1), 53-61.

Davidson, R. J., & Begley, S. (2012). The emotional life of your brain:

How its unique patterns affect the way you think, feel, and live—and how you can change them. Hudson Street Press.

Dweck, C. S. (2006). Mindset: The new psychology of success. Random House.

Frankl, V. E. (1946). Man's search for meaning. Beacon Press.

Fredrickson, B. L. (2013). Love 2.0: How our supreme emotion affects everything we feel, think, do, and become. Hudson Street Press.

Goyal, M., Singh, S., Sibinga, E. M., Gould, N. F., Rowland-Seymour, A., Sharma, R., ... & Haythornthwaite, J. A. (2014). Meditation programs for psychological stress and well-being: A systematic review and meta-analysis. JAMA Internal Medicine, 174(3), 357-368.

Hanson, R. (2013). Hardwiring happiness: The new brain science of contentment, calm, and confidence. Harmony.

Ivtzan, I., Chan, C. P., Gardner, H. E., & Prashar, K. (2013). Linking religion and spirituality with psychological well-being: Examining self-actualisation, meaning in life, and personal growth initiative. Journal of Religion and Health, 52(3), 915-929.

Kabat-Zinn, J. (1994). Wherever you go, there you are: Mindfulness meditation in everyday life. Hyperion.

Keltner, D. (2016). The power paradox: How we gain and lose influence. Penguin Press.

Kramer, A. D., Guillory, J. E., & Hancock, J. T. (2014). Experimental evidence of massive-scale emotional contagion through social networks. Proceedings of the National Academy of Sciences, 111(24), 8788-8790.

Lebedev, A. V., Kaelen, M., Lövdén, M., Nilsson, J., Feilding, A., Nutt, D. J., & Carhart-Harris, R. L. (2020). LSD-induced entropic brain activity predicts subsequent personality change. Human Brain Mapping, 41(8), 2124-2140.

MacLean, K. A., Ferrer, E., Aichele, S. R., Bridwell, D. A., Zanesco, A. P., Jacobs, T. L., ... & Saron, C. D. (2010). Intensive meditation training improves perceptual discrimination and sustained attention.

Psychological Science, 21(6), 829-839.

Mayer, F. S., Frantz, C. M., Bruehlman-Senecal, E., & Dolliver, K. (2009). Why is nature beneficial? The role of connectedness to nature. Environment and Behavior, 41(5), 607-643.

Miller, L. (2015). The spiritual child: The new science on parenting for health and lifelong thriving. St. Martin's Press.

Neff, K. D. (2003). The development and validation of a scale to measure self-compassion. Self and Identity, 2(3), 223-250.

Park, C. L. (2010). Making sense of the meaning literature: An integrative review of meaning making and its effects on adjustment to stressful life events. Psychological Bulletin, 136(2), 257-301.

Park, C. L. (2013). The meaning making model: A framework for understanding meaning, spirituality, and stress-related growth in health psychology. European Health Psychologist, 15(2), 40-47.

Puchalski, C. M., Ferrell, B., Virani, R., Otis-Green, S., Baird, P., Bull, J., ... & Sulmasy, D. (2009). Improving the quality of spiritual care as a dimension of palliative care: The report of the Consensus Conference. Journal of Palliative Medicine, 12(10), 885-904.

Rudd, M., Vohs, K. D., & Aaker, J. (2012). Awe expands people's perception of time, alters decision making, and enhances well-being. Psychological Science, 23(10), 1130-1136.

Schwartz, S. H., & Sortheix, F. M. (2018). Values and subjective well-being. In E. Diener, S. Oishi, & L. Tay (Eds.), Handbook of well-being. DEF Publishers.

Sheldon, K. M., & Elliot, A. J. (1999). Goal striving, need satisfaction, and longitudinal well-being: The self-concordance model. Journal of Personality and Social Psychology, 76(3), 482-497.

Smith, E. E. (2017). The power of meaning: Crafting a life that matters. Crown.

Tang, Y. Y., Hölzel, B. K., & Posner, M. I. (2015). The neuroscience of mindfulness meditation. Nature Reviews Neuroscience, 16(4), 213-225.

Tarr, B., Launay, J., & Dunbar, R. I. (2015). Synchrony and exertion during dance independently raise pain threshold and encourage social bonding. Biology Letters, 11(10), 20150767.

Trapnell, P. D., & Campbell, J. D. (1999). Private self-consciousness and the five-factor model of personality: Distinguishing rumination from reflection. Journal of Personality and Social Psychology, 76(2), 284-304.

Van Cappellen, P., & Saroglou, V. (2012). Awe activates religious and spiritual feelings and behavioral intentions. Psychology of Religion and Spirituality, 4(3), 223-236.

Wink, P., & Dillon, M. (2003). Religiousness, spirituality, and psychosocial functioning in late adulthood: Findings from a longitudinal study. Psychology and Aging, 18(4), 916-924.

Xu, W., Oei, T. P., Liu, X., Wang, X., & Ding, C. (2016). The moderating and mediating roles of self-acceptance and tolerance to others in the relationship between mindfulness and subjective well-being. Journal of Health Psychology, 21(7), 1446-1456.

22

Sources Chapter 11:

Cited Sources:

Adams, K. (1999). A brief history of journal writing. The Illustrated Encyclopedia of Mind-Body Medicine, 1, 546-547.

Amabile, T. M., & Kramer, S. J. (2011). The progress principle: Using small wins to ignite joy, engagement, and creativity at work. Harvard Business Review Press.

Beghetto, R. A. (2014). Creative mortification: An initial exploration. Psychology of Aesthetics, Creativity, and the Arts, 8(3), 266-276.

Blomdahl, C., Gunnarsson, A. B., Guregård, S., & Björklund, A. (2013). A realist review of art therapy for clients with depression. The Arts in Psychotherapy, 40(3), 322-330.

Botella, M., Glaveanu, V., Zenasni, F., Storme, M., Myszkowski, N., Wolff, M., & Lubart, T. (2018). How artists create: Creative process and multivariate factors. Learning and Individual Differences, 26, 161-170.

Carson, S. H. (2010). Your creative brain: Seven steps to maximize imagination, productivity, and innovation in your life. Jossey-Bass.

Conner, T. S., DeYoung, C. G., & Silvia, P. J. (2018). Everyday creative activity as a path to flourishing. The Journal of Positive Psychology,

13(2), 181-189.

D'Amico, M., Lalonde, C., & Snow, S. (2015). Evaluating the efficacy of drama therapy in teaching social skills to children with Autism Spectrum Disorders. Drama Therapy Review, 1(1), 21-39.

Erkkilä, J., Punkanen, M., Fachner, J., Ala-Ruona, E., Pöntiö, I., Tervaniemi, M., ... & Gold, C. (2011). Individual music therapy for depression: Randomised controlled trial. The British Journal of Psychiatry, 199(2), 132-139.

Eschleman, K. J., Madsen, J., Alarcon, G., & Barelka, A. (2014). Benefiting from creative activity: The positive relationships between creative activity, recovery experiences, and performance-related outcomes. Journal of Occupational and Organizational Psychology, 87(3), 579-598.

Kaimal, G., Ray, K., & Muniz, J. (2016). Reduction of cortisol levels and participants' responses following art making. Art Therapy, 33(2), 74-80.

Kaimal, G. (2019). Adaptive response theory: An evolutionary framework for clinical research in art therapy. Art Therapy, 36(4), 215-219.

Kaufman, J. C. (2018). Creativity as a stepping stone toward a brighter future. Journal of Intelligence, 6(2), 21.

Kaufman, S. B. (2013). Ungifted: Intelligence redefined. Basic Books.

Koch, S., Kunz, T., Lykou, S., & Cruz, R. (2019). Effects of dance movement therapy and dance on health-related psychological outcomes: A meta-analysis. The Arts in Psychotherapy, 41(1), 46-64.

Lebuda, I., Zabelina, D. L., & Karwowski, M. (2016). Mind full of ideas: A meta-analysis of the mindfulness–creativity link. Personality and Individual Differences, 93, 22-26.

Lowe, G. (2006). Health-related effects of creative and expressive writing. Health Education, 106(1), 60-70.

Malchiodi, C. A. (2020). Trauma and expressive arts therapy: Brain, body, and imagination in the healing process. Guilford Publications.

McCoy, J. M., & Evans, G. W. (2002). The potential role of the physical environment in fostering creativity. Creativity Research Journal, 14(3-4), 409-426.

Moreau, C. P., & Dahl, D. W. (2005). Designing the solution: The impact of constraints on consumers' creativity. Journal of Consumer Research, 32(1), 13-22.

Palmiero, M., Di Giacomo, D., & Passafiume, D. (2016). Can creativity predict cognitive reserve? The Journal of Creative Behavior, 50(1), 7-23.

Pennebaker, J. W. (1997). Writing about emotional experiences as a therapeutic process. Psychological Science, 8(3), 162-166.

Richards, R. (2007). Everyday creativity: Our hidden potential. In R. Richards (Ed.), Everyday creativity and new views of human nature: Psychological, social, and spiritual perspectives (pp. 25-54). American Psychological Association.

Shalley, C. E. (1995). Effects of coaction, expected evaluation, and goal setting on creativity and productivity. Academy of Management Journal, 38(2), 483-503.

Sloan, D. M., Marx, B. P., Bovin, M. J., Feinstein, B. A., & Gallagher, M. W. (2011). Written exposure as an intervention for PTSD: A randomized clinical trial with motor vehicle accident survivors. Behaviour Research and Therapy, 50(10), 627-635.

Strang, C. (2018). The healing power of art. American Art Therapy Association.

Sun, J., Chen, Q., Zhang, Q., Li, Y., Li, H., Wei, D., ... & Qiu, J. (2016). Training your brain to be more creative: Brain functional and structural changes induced by divergent thinking training. Human Brain Mapping, 37(10), 3375-3387.

Thayer, R. E., & Lane, R. D. (2000). A model of neurovisceral integration in emotion regulation and dysregulation. Journal of Affective Disorders, 61(3), 201-216.

23

Sources Chapter 12:

Cited Sources:

Amabile, T. M., & Kramer, S. J. (2011). The power of small wins. Harvard Business Review, 89(5), 70-80.

Ariga, A., & Lleras, A. (2011). Brief and rare mental "breaks" keep you focused: Deactivation and reactivation of task goals preempt vigilance decrements. Cognition, 118(3), 439-443.

Ashford, S. J., & Cummings, L. L. (1983). Feedback as an individual resource: Personal strategies of creating information. Organizational Behavior and Human Performance, 32(3), 370-398.

Beauregard, T. A., & Henry, L. C. (2009). Making the link between work-life balance practices and organizational performance. Human Resource Management Review, 19(1), 9-22.

Brown, B. (2010). The gifts of imperfection: Let go of who you think you're supposed to be and embrace who you are. Hazelden Publishing.

Chiaburu, D. S., & Harrison, D. A. (2008). Do peers make the place? Conceptual synthesis and meta-analysis of coworker effects on perceptions, attitudes, OCBs, and performance. Journal of Applied Psychology, 93(5), 1082-1103.

Church, A. H. (1997). Managerial self-awareness in high-performing individuals in organizations. Journal of Applied Psychology, 82(2), 281-292.

Coulson, J. C., McKenna, J., & Field, M. (2008). Exercising at work and self-reported work performance. International Journal of Workplace Health Management, 1(3), 176-197.

Crum, A. J., Salovey, P., & Achor, S. (2013). Rethinking stress: The role of mindsets in determining the stress response. Journal of Personality and Social Psychology, 104(4), 716-733.

De Vos, A., De Hauw, S., & Van der Heijden, B. I. (2011). Competency development and career success: The mediating role of employability. Journal of Vocational Behavior, 79(2), 438-447.

DeRue, D. S., Nahrgang, J. D., Hollenbeck, J. R., & Workman, K. (2012). A quasi-experimental study of after-event reviews and leadership development. Journal of Applied Psychology, 97(5), 997-1015.

Dweck, C. S. (2006). Mindset: The new psychology of success. Random House.

Eby, L. T., Allen, T. D., Evans, S. C., Ng, T., & DuBois, D. L. (2008). Does mentoring matter? A multidisciplinary meta-analysis comparing mentored and non-mentored individuals. Journal of Vocational Behavior, 72(2), 254-267.

Edmondson, A. (1999). Psychological safety and learning behavior in work teams. Administrative Science Quarterly, 44(2), 350-383.

Grant, A. M. (2013). Give and take: A revolutionary approach to success. Viking.

Häfner, A., & Stock, A. (2010). Time management training and perceived control of time at work. The Journal of Psychology, 144(5), 429-447.

Humphrey, S. E., Nahrgang, J. D., & Morgeson, F. P. (2007). Integrating motivational, social, and contextual work design features: A meta-analytic summary and theoretical extension of the work design literature. Journal of Applied Psychology, 92(5), 1332-1356.

Kets de Vries, M. F. R. (2014). Mindful leadership coaching: Journeys into the interior. Palgrave Macmillan.

Locke, E. A., & Latham, G. P. (2002). Building a practically useful theory of goal setting and task motivation: A 35-year odyssey. American Psychologist, 57(9), 705-717.

Maslach, C., Schaufeli, W. B., & Leiter, M. P. (2001). Job burnout. Annual Review of Psychology, 52(1), 397-422.

Neff, K. D., Hsieh, Y. P., & Dejitterat, K. (2005). Self-compassion, achievement goals, and coping with academic failure. Self and Identity, 4(3), 263-287.

Ng, T. W., & Feldman, D. C. (2012). Employee voice behavior: A meta-analytic test of the conservation of resources framework. Journal of Organizational Behavior, 33(2), 216-234.

Rhoades, L., & Eisenberger, R. (2002). Perceived organizational support: A review of the literature. Journal of Applied Psychology, 87(4), 698-714.

Sapolsky, R. M. (2004). Why zebras don't get ulcers: The acclaimed guide to stress, stress-related diseases, and coping. Holt Paperbacks.

Senge, P. M. (1990). The fifth discipline: The art and practice of the learning organization. Doubleday/Currency.

Sonnentag, S. (2012). Psychological detachment from work during leisure time: The benefits of mentally disengaging from work. Current Directions in Psychological Science, 21(2), 114-118.

Sonnentag, S., Binnewies, C., & Mojza, E. J. (2010). Staying well and engaged when demands are high: The role of psychological detachment. Journal of Applied Psychology, 95(5), 965-976.

Welsh, D. T., & Ordóñez, L. D. (2014). The dark side of consecutive high-performance goals: Linking goal setting, depletion, and unethical behavior. Organizational Behavior and Human Decision Processes, 123(2), 79-89.

Wolever, R. Q., Bobinet, K. J., McCabe, K., Mackenzie, E. R., Fekete, E., Kusnick, C. A., & Baime, M. (2012). Effective and viable mind–body stress reduction in the workplace: A randomized controlled trial. Journal of Occupational Health Psychology, 17(2), 246-258.

Wolff, H. G., & Moser, K. (2009). Effects of networking on career success: A longitudinal study. Journal of Applied Psychology, 94(1), 196-206.

24

Sources Chapter 13:

Cited Sources:

Ashford, S. J., & Cummings, L. L. (1983). Feedback as an individual resource: Personal strategies of creating information. Organizational Behavior and Human Performance, 32(3), 370-398.

Bolton, G., Howlett, S., Lago, C., & Wright, J. K. (2004). Writing cures: An introductory handbook of writing in counselling and therapy. Routledge.

Bonanno, G. A., & Burton, C. L. (2013). Regulatory flexibility: An individual differences perspective on coping and emotion regulation. Perspectives on Psychological Science, 8(6), 591-612.

Breines, J. G., & Chen, S. (2012). Self-compassion increases self-improvement motivation. Personality and Social Psychology Bulletin, 38(9), 1133-1143.

Carstensen, L. L. (2006). The influence of a sense of time on human development. Science, 312(5782), 1913-1915.

Castonguay, L. G., Boswell, J. F., Constantino, M. J., Goldfried, M. R., & Hill, C. E. (2010). Training implications of harmful effects of psychological treatments. American Psychologist, 65(1), 34-49.

Conley, C. S., Travers, L. V., & Bryant, F. B. (2013). Promoting psychosocial adjustment and stress management in first-year college students: The benefits of engagement in a psychosocial wellness seminar. Journal of American College Health, 61(2), 75-86.

D'Souza, F., Egan, S. J., & Rees, C. S. (2011). The relationship between perfectionism, stress and burnout in clinical psychologists. Behaviour Change, 28(1), 17-28.

Duckworth, A. (2016). Grit: The power of passion and perseverance. Scribner.

Dweck, C. S. (2006). Mindset: The new psychology of success. Random House.

Fogg, B. J. (2019). Tiny habits: The small changes that change everything. Houghton Mifflin Harcourt.

Folkman, S., & Moskowitz, J. T. (2004). Coping: Pitfalls and promise. Annual Review of Psychology, 55, 745-774.

Gollwitzer, P. M., & Sheeran, P. (2006). Implementation intentions and goal achievement: A meta-analysis of effects and processes. Advances in Experimental Social Psychology, 38, 69-119.

Häfner, A., & Stock, A. (2010). Time management training and perceived control of time at work. The Journal of Psychology, 144(5), 429-447.

Huppert, F. A., & So, T. T. (2013). Flourishing across Europe: Application of a new conceptual framework for defining well-being. Social Indicators Research, 110(3), 837-861.

Kashdan, T. B., & Silvia, P. J. (2009). Curiosity and interest: The benefits of thriving on novelty and challenge. In S. J. Lopez & C. R. Snyder (Eds.), Oxford handbook of positive psychology (pp. 367-374). Oxford University Press.

Korb, A. (2015). The upward spiral: Using neuroscience to reverse the course of depression, one small change at a time. New Harbinger Publications.

Lally, P., Van Jaarsveld, C. H., Potts, H. W., & Wardle, J. (2010). How are habits formed: Modelling habit formation in the real world. European Journal of Social Psychology, 40(6), 998-1009.

Locke, E. A., & Latham, G. P. (2002). Building a practically useful theory of goal setting and task motivation: A 35-year odyssey. American Psychologist, 57(9), 705-717.

Lum, T. Y., & Lightfoot, E. (2005). The effects of volunteering on the physical and mental health of older people. Research on Aging, 27(1), 31-55.

McGonigal, K. (2013). The willpower instinct: How self-control works, why it matters, and what you can do to get more of it. Avery.

Murthy, V. (2020). Together: The healing power of human connection in a sometimes-lonely world. Harper Wave.

Myers, S. B., Sweeney, A. C., Popick, V., Wesley, K., Bordfeld, A., & Fingerhut, R. (2012). Self-care practices and perceived stress levels among psychology graduate students. Training and Education in Professional Psychology, 6(1), 55-66.

Neff, K. D. (2011). Self-compassion, self-esteem, and well-being. Social and Personality Psychology Compass, 5(1), 1-12.

Nelson, S. K., Kushlev, K., & Lyubomirsky, S. (2014). The pains and pleasures of parenting: When, why, and how is parenthood associated with more or less well-being? Psychological Bulletin, 140(3), 846-895.

Patel, M. S., Asch, D. A., & Volpp, K. G. (2015). Wearable devices as facilitators, not drivers, of health behavior change. JAMA, 313(5), 459-460.

Sheldon, K. M., & Elliot, A. J. (1999). Goal striving, need satisfaction, and longitudinal well-being: The self-concordance model. Journal of Personality and Social Psychology, 76(3), 482-497.

Sonnentag, S. (2012). Psychological detachment from work during leisure time: The benefits of mentally disengaging from work. Current Directions in Psychological Science, 21(2), 114-118.

Trapnell, P. D., & Campbell, J. D. (1999). Private self-consciousness and the five-factor model of personality: Distinguishing rumination from reflection. Journal of Personality and Social Psychology, 76(2), 284-304.

Wang, H. X., Jin, Y., Hendrie, H. C., Liang, C., Yang, L., Cheng, Y., ... & Gao, S. (2013). Late life leisure activities and risk of cognitive decline. Journals of Gerontology Series A: Biomedical Sciences and Medical Sciences, 68(2), 205-213.

Wood, W., & Neal, D. T. (2007). A new look at habits and the habit-goal interface. Psychological Review, 114(4), 843-863.

Conclusion:

Brown, B. (2018). Dare to lead: Brave work. Tough conversations. Whole hearts. Random House.

Fishbach, A., & Dhar, R. (2005). Goals as excuses or guides: The liberating effect of perceived goal progress on choice. Journal of Consumer Research, 32(3), 370-377.

Ellis, S., Carette, B., Anseel, F., & Lievens, F. (2014). Systematic reflection: Implications for learning from failures and successes. Current Directions in Psychological Science, 23(1), 67-72.

Gilovich, T., & Ross, L. (2015). The wisest one in the room: How you can benefit from social psychology's most powerful insights. Free Press.

Gollwitzer, P. M., & Sheeran, P. (2006). Implementation intentions and goal achievement: A meta-analysis of effects and processes. Advances in Experimental Social Psychology, 38, 69-119.

Guttman, J. (2020). Beyond happiness: The trap of happiness and how to find deeper meaning and joy. G.P. Putnam's Sons.

Hanson, R. (2013). Hardwiring happiness: The new brain science of contentment, calm, and confidence. Harmony.

Keyes, C. L., & Simoes, E. J. (2012). To flourish or not: Positive mental health and all-cause mortality. American Journal of Public Health, 102(11), 2164-2172.

Neff, K. D. (2011). Self-compassion, self-esteem, and well-being. Social and Personality Psychology Compass, 5(1), 1-12.

Neff, K. D., & Beretvas, S. N. (2013). The role of self-compassion in romantic relationships. Self and Identity, 12(1), 78-98.

Roepke, A. M., Jayawickreme, E., & Riffle, O. M. (2013). Meaning and health: A systematic review. Applied Research in Quality of Life, 9(4), 1055-1079.

Seppälä, E. (2016). The happiness track: How to apply the science of happiness to accelerate your success. HarperOne.

Shapiro, S. L. (2020). Good morning, I love you: Mindfulness and self-compassion practices to rewire your brain for calm, clarity, and joy. Sounds True.

Sonnentag, S. (2003). Recovery, work engagement, and proactive behavior: A new look at the interface between nonwork and work. Journal of Applied Psychology, 88(3), 518-528.

Umberson, D., Crosnoe, R., & Reczek, C. (2010). Social relationships and health behavior across the life course. Annual Review of Sociology, 36, 139-157.

Wickrama, K. A. S., Conger, R. D., Wallace, L. E., & Elder Jr, G. H. (1999). The intergenerational transmission of health-risk behaviors: Adolescent lifestyles and gender moderating effects. Journal of Health and Social Behavior, 40(3), 258-272.

Resources:

Bakker, D., & Rickard, N. (2018). Engagement in mobile phone app for self-monitoring of emotional wellbeing predicts changes in mental health: MoodPrism. Journal of Affective Disorders, 227, 432-442.

Cohen, S., Kamarck, T., & Mermelstein, R. (1983). A global measure of perceived stress. Journal of Health and Social Behavior, 24(4), 385-396.

Cook-Cottone, C. P. (2015). Mindfulness and yoga for self-regulation: A primer for mental health professionals. Springer Publishing Company.

Feehan, L. M., Geldman, J., Sayre, E. C., Park, C., Ezzat, A. M., Yoo, J. Y.,

... & Li, L. C. (2018). Accuracy of Fitbit devices: Systematic review and narrative syntheses of quantitative data. JMIR mHealth and uHealth, 6(8), e10527.

Hettler, B. (1976). The six dimensions of wellness model. National Wellness Institute.

Howells, A., Ivtzan, I., & Eiroa-Orosa, F. J. (2016). Putting the 'app' in happiness: A randomised controlled trial of a smartphone-based mindfulness intervention to enhance wellbeing. Journal of Happiness Studies, 17(1), 163-185.

Huberty, J., Green, J., Glissmann, C., Larkey, L., Puzia, M., & Lee, C. (2021). Efficacy of the mindfulness meditation mobile app "Calm" to reduce stress among college students: Randomized controlled trial. JMIR mHealth and uHealth, 9(6), e25532.

Jacobs, S., Radnitz, C., & Hildebrandt, T. (2017). Adherence as a predictor of weight loss in a commonly used smartphone application. Obesity Research & Clinical Practice, 11(2), 206-214.

Korb, A. (2015). The upward spiral: Using neuroscience to reverse the course of depression, one small change at a time. New Harbinger Publications.

Neff, K. D. (2003). The development and validation of a scale to measure self-compassion. Self and Identity, 2(3), 223-250.

Rickard, N., Arjmand, H. A., Bakker, D., & Seabrook, E. (2016). Development of a mobile phone app to support self-monitoring of emotional well-being: A mental health digital innovation. JMIR Mental Health, 3(4), e49.

Saakvitne, K. W., & Pearlman, L. A. (1996). Transforming the pain: A workbook on vicarious traumatization. W. W. Norton & Company.

Stamm, B. H. (2010). The concise ProQOL manual. Pocatello, ID: ProQOL.org.

Torous, J., Firth, J., Huckvale, K., Larsen, M. E., Cosco, T. D., Carney, R., ... & Christensen, H. (2018). The emerging imperative for a consensus approach toward the rating and clinical recommendation of mental health apps. The Journal of Nervous and Mental Disease, 206(8), 662–666.

135

www.ingramcontent.com/pod-product-compliance
Lightning Source LLC
Chambersburg PA
CBHW071328140726
47996CB00005B/1882